THE TAKE THAT FACT FILE 2

Rick Sky is one of Britain's top music journalists and has interviewed almost all the major rock stars. He has edited the daily pop and showbiz column of the *Daily Star*, the *Sun* and most recently, the *Daily Mirror*. He is now freelance and has contributed to dozens of publications around the world, including *Spin,* the *Chicago Tribune* and *Max*. He is the author of *The Take That Fact File, The Show Must Go On* and *Michael Jackson: The Bad Year*. As an authority on Take That he has appeared on numerous TV and radio shows, including ITN News, Talk Radio, GMTV and Sky TV.

THE TAKE THAT *fact file 2*

RICK SKY

Illustrations by Andy Hunt

HarperCollins*Publishers*

HarperCollins*Publishers*
77–85 Fulham Palace Road,
Hammersmith, London W6 8JB

This paperback edition 1995
1 3 5 7 9 8 6 4 2

First edition published in paperback by Grafton 1993
Reprinted nine times

ISBN 0 00638774 8

Set in Melior and Futura by
Rowland Phototypesetting Ltd,
Bury St Edmunds, Suffolk

Printed in Great Britain by
HarperCollinsManufacturing Glasgow

For Take That fans everywhere.

The author and the publishers would like to thank the following photographers and picture agencies for allowing us to reproduce their photographs:

Xavier Pictures Ltd
Retna Pictures
All Action
London Features International Ltd
Famous
Rex

CONTENTS

IN THE BEGINNING

The early days of Take That

It was a week before Christmas and Gary Barlow's dad wanted to buy his ten-year-old son a really special present. BMX bikes were all the rage that year but Gary's dad also noticed how obsessed by pop the blond-haired youngster was.

Colin Barlow was in a dilemma – he wanted the present to be a surprise but he didn't want it to be the wrong kind of surprise, so in the end he decided to let Gary choose for himself. He told him he could either have a bike or a small keyboard.

Gary plumped for the keyboard and it was a decision that would one day change his life. It was the decision that sowed the seeds for what has become Britain's most successful teenage group since Duran Duran – Take That. For Gary was a natural musician and within a year, at the tender age of eleven, he was already playing the organ in a cabaret band where most of the other group members were in their fifties.

But even at that age, Gary dreamed of bigger and

better things. One of his greatest inspirations was the flamboyant pop star Adam Ant, who had launched himself from the remnants of the British punk scene as one of pop music's most adventurous creations.

Little Gary was transfixed. 'One day,' he mused to himself, 'I'd like to be a pop star. One day I'd like to be just like Adam Ant.' Though many people thought Adam Ant was a manufactured pop star, he wasn't at all. The songs he sang, including 'Prince Charming' and 'Stand and Deliver', were his own compositions. That struck home to young Gary – he didn't just want to be a pop star, he wanted to be a pop star who could sing his own songs.

'I loved Adam Ant. I loved his image,' says Gary. 'I think he was so appealing to youngsters. At school I put together a band with a couple of my mates that was a copy of Adam and the Ants. They had this fantastically hypnotic drum beat and we copied it by drumming on these huge biscuit tins while I sang Adam's songs over the top. That's what really started me off. I also loved the Beatles. I used to put their records on and just mime to them all day long.'

And just as Gary had a natural aptitude for the keyboard, he also had a remarkable talent for

composing his own songs. His first complete songs were written at the age of thirteen and just a few years later they were tried out in his very own fledgling band, The Cutest Rush, the band that he formed with the second Take That member Mark Owen. Recalls Mark: 'I was looking for work as a singer and met up with Gary. I was just knocked out by what a brilliant keyboard player he was.'

He was more than brilliant – Gary was a man in a hurry who was already showing an extraordinary talent for writing songs.

'Before Take That was formed I already had about fifty songs written,' says Gary. 'Sometimes I used to set myself the task of writing and recording a song a day. But often the songs happened quicker than that, much quicker. "A Million Love Songs", for instance, was written in about five or six minutes when I was fifteen.

'I was very proud of it but not everyone shared my confidence. A few months after I had written it, I took it along to a music publisher to see what they thought of it. They rejected it. They said it had to be much better and much stronger to stand a chance of being published.

'Another publisher I took it to was even more brutal and cruel. I took along a tape which included that song, a tape that I had slaved over for months, getting it to what I thought was perfect. I am not going to say the name of the company I went to, but after the guy had listened to it, he took it out of the machine and then hurled it out of the window into the street below. Then he told me never to come back. I couldn't believe what he had done. It was so horrible. I was totally devastated.

'When I think back to those days it makes me laugh. The song that they turned down was exactly the same song that we had such a huge hit with. I didn't change a line.'

Mark Owen was only thirteen years old when he met up with Gary in Manchester's famous Strawberry Studios. Gary had been awarded some recording time in the studio when he won the BBC's annual 'Carol For Christmas' competition. Mark had an after-school job there.

Much of their free time was spent up in Gary's bedroom, which boasted a portable four-track recording studio where Gary was writing the songs that would one day make Take That famous. Gary was working on the cabaret circuit doing cover versions of classic hit songs but teaming up with Mark was the spur he needed to kickstart his own pop career. After forming their band, The Cutest Rush, they decided they needed to find some work

so, armed with a demo tape, they went along to the entertainment agency run by Nigel Martin-Smith.

A few months later two more fresh-faced teenagers, Howard Donald and Jason Orange, turned up at Martin-Smith's agency. The two had been in rival Manchester break-dance groups until they decided to join forces and form their own dance group, Street Beat. Break-dancing was the most athletic type of dancing the pop world had ever seen. Originally developed on the streets of New York, the dancers were nothing short of disco acrobats, performing somersaults, backflips and headspins in the hope of earning some money from the astounded passers-by.

Howard and Jason were ambitious and took their form of disco busking into the local clubs where they would be paid £25 a night for their fancy flips and spins. Jason's dancing already had a wide audience as he appeared regularly on Pete Waterman's late-night TV show, *The Hitman and Her*. And it was during one of the shows that Jason first met up with Martin-Smith.

'Break-dancing was something that a lot of kids did because it kept them out of trouble on the streets,' says Jason. 'It was a big craze for a couple of years around 1983 and I got really into it. I wanted to be a dancer more than anything else. I didn't really want to be in a pop group. I dreamed about dancing in front of thousands of people and really putting on a spectacular show.'

When Jason and Howard strolled into Martin-Smith's office that warm summer day they were looking for advice. They wanted some help in their dancing career and thought Nigel might be just the man to guide them. But Nigel had other ideas. He had a brainwave – he put two and two together and got a group. Howard and Jason were the perfect pair to team up with those two other youngsters, Gary and Mark, who had come to him earlier. And so Take That was conceived.

But Martin-Smith wasn't quite satisfied. He thought the foursome lacked one thing – a fifth member. And he already had an idea of who it might be. A Stoke-on-Trent lad Robbie Williams, who had high hopes of becoming an actor, had just signed up with the agency and Nigel thought he would be perfect. Robbie met the rest of the band and went along for his audition. The others took to him straight away and so Take That was complete.

The formation of Take That was a dream that Martin-Smith had long nurtured. A vision of the perfect teen group had constantly invaded his everyday business thoughts. He had set himself the strictest of standards – he wanted all the

members of the group to be talented, good-looking, energetic and totally committed. With the creation of Take That he believed he had such a band.

One thing that immediately singled his group out was just how young they were – Robbie was only sixteen, Mark just eighteen, Gary a year older, Jason twenty and Howard twenty-two. When they signed their contract with Martin-Smith in September 1990 he insisted that some of their parents were there, too. Marjorie Barlow was impressed when Nigel advised Gary to bring along a parent. 'You hear so many things about the crookedness of the music business and about bad management, and he wanted to set everybody's mind at ease and show that everything was above board.'

A year of hope and hardship, delight and despair was to follow the signing of that contract. The first thing they did was sit down with manager Nigel Martin-Smith and talk about how they were going to take on the pop world. They talked almost daily for the first few months about the songs they were going to sing, the act they were going to perform and the image they wanted. It was a period where they did little more than practise, talk and dream. 'Really the band was nothing for those first six months,' recalls Gary. 'It was a very odd period. We had all come together because Marky and myself were looking for management, then we were hooked up with Jason and Howard and finally Robbie. We were then told to go off and see if we could write something or come up with anything. It was very off-the-cuff stuff.

'Nigel was originally interested in my writing and when we first met I thought he was going to get me a publishing deal because that's what we always spoke about. For a long time the band just didn't seem real.'

But the band most certainly was real and the first thing they needed to prove they existed was a name. The problem was solved one day when the guys saw a picture of pop superstar Madonna. 'It was a very raunchy picture of Madonna,' remembers Mark, 'above which was written the caption "Take That". We had spent weeks agonizing over a name, but this just struck all of us. We thought it was snappy and had a punch to it.

'At first we decided to call ourselves Take That and Party, but we dropped the "Party" bit when we heard about the American group The Party. We knew we had something original to offer and we wanted to make sure our name was original, too.'

They had chosen their name – next came their image. They found their first look courtesy of the fashionable shopping district on Kensington High

Street, London. It was Jason who chose it for them. 'We were on our way to Hyper Hyper when we walked past this leather shop and Jason saw this jacket with tassels hanging off it that he really wanted,' says Mark. 'So he went off and bought it. And then the whole group had to find jackets that matched it.'

Early publicity pictures of Take That show the band wearing sequinned codpieces over tight leather trousers. It was a strange mix, part wholesomeness and part danger. It was a style they would later ditch when they decided that the mean and tough leather look was too much at odds with their clean-cut image. Nick Wilson, former executive producer with *The Hitman and Her*, who gave the band one of their first breaks on the popular TV show, remembers the original look: 'The boys always wore leather jackets in the early days. But as far as I can recall, their success happened when they took all that leather gear off and started to look more like they do in real life. They blossomed when they appeared like a bunch of normal lads.

'I suspect they had some misguided image-building in the beginning.'

Today Gary won't be drawn into admitting that their fetish-style leather was a mistake: 'I don't know if it was. We're here now because of all the things that happened to us in the early days. It's hard to know what was a mistake and what was a plus. I mean, I must admit I look back now and think "oh no" about the way I looked in all that leather and the way I used to have my hair. But they were fun times for us then. We all enjoyed it and even though we didn't have any hits we were getting our name around and getting recognized; so I don't really regret anything from that time.'

The leather look was showcased at the band's very first show in the nearby Lancashire town of Huddersfield. 'There were about twenty people in the audience and a dog,' remembers Gary. 'Only about ten of them were watching but to be honest I was glad because I felt I was messing a lot of things up. We really didn't care that only a few people had bothered to see us. It was our first gig and we were just so excited about performing that it wouldn't have mattered if only the dog was watching. Besides, we didn't notice the audience, we were much too busy concentrating on the songs, the music and our dance steps. Afterwards we were on such a high.'

Twenty people and a dog might not be the stuff that pop legends are made of, but it was at least a beginning.

*

Shortly after this the band had a wonderful stroke of luck – a TV appearance. It was a great break. Some bands wait years to get a slot on a TV show and some never manage to get one at all. Yet here was a band who had only just been formed on a programme that could bring their music to millions.

That first appearance was on a music show called *Cool Cube*, a programme on the now defunct satellite channel BSB.

It was the television appearance that finally convinced Gary that the band were not a figment of somebody's imagination but real flesh and blood: 'It all changed when Nigel came along one day and said that he thought we had a chance of doing some TV and we should get something together for it. I wrote a song called "Waiting Around" and took it to the other lads. They thought it was good and devised a bit of a routine. Then we showed it to Nigel. He liked it and then sprung another surprise – he said we needed two songs because that was probably what the TV programme would ask us to do. So, I had to rush away and dash off another song, called "Girl", and the rest of the guys had to quickly get together another routine.'

Former *Cool Cube* producer Ro Newton recalls: 'Nigel contacted me and said he had this really good band for the programme and he asked me what the chance was of getting them on the show. He brought the lads in to meet me and I was very impressed – they had a great dance routine and smashing voices. They appeared on the show a few times because they were so popular and we had such a great response to them.'

The band were determined to cause a sensation on the shows. On one occasion they wore red velvet bomber jackets and excruciatingly tight black cycling shorts which didn't leave much to the imagination. 'We were a little dubious about the tight cycling shorts in the beginning,' says Ro. 'They were rather risqué.'

From the very beginning, Nigel Martin-Smith was the driving force behind the band, constantly encouraging and motivating them to always give their best shot at everything.

Ro, a former *Smash Hits* journalist, saw Nigel in action: 'Before their first TV appearance Nigel gave them a real pep talk like a coach in a dressing room before a big match. The boys appeared a bit apprehensive because it was their first show. But they never showed any signs of being cocky, they were always eager to please. At times Nigel appeared like a father towards the band as he was very protective of them. But he was also strict with

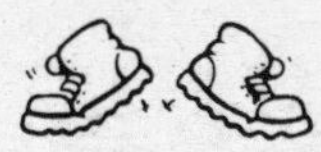

them and would have a go if he thought they looked sloppy or weren't working hard enough. Sometimes I thought he was too hard on them because they did push themselves.'

After appearing on *Cool Cube* the band went on to star on *The Hitman and Her.* It was another big break for them. The show, which had fast become a must for all young dance fans, was the brainchild of pop mogul Pete Waterman. Affable, motor-mouthed Waterman hosted the show himself together with pretty TV presenter Michaela Strachan. It was fast, played the latest dance songs and was above all fun. And it was a great place to check out fresh, new talent. Gary acknowledges what an important show it was for the novice band to do: 'When we did the *Hitman*, all of a sudden everyone started getting interested in us. It was so exciting. We set up a few gigs and started doing them.'

Former producer of *The Hitman and Her* Angie Smith remembers the band very well. 'When I first met Take That I thought they looked like five good-looking boys from next door. The teenage girls loved them as they appeared so accessible, not like Prince or Michael Jackson.

'I remember when they appeared on the show they performed their debut single, "Do What U Like", which caused a real stir.'

TV appearances are important to a new band but even more so is a video. The band knew they had to get a video for their first single that would get them noticed, that would stand out from the hundreds of videos that are released every week. In the end their very first video did more than get their faces on TV – it got their bare behinds on film, too.

The video for 'Do What U Like' was shot in one day in Stockport and it revolved around jelly, dance routines and the band's naked bottoms. Co-producers Ro Newton and Angie Smith were brought in, on a tight budget, to make the video.

'When we had our first meeting with the band we went to a rehearsal room in Manchester and they showed us their dance routine,' says Angie. 'I thought they were absolutely brilliant and as far as I was concerned they had the makings of the perfect pop band. They all looked very good and they were excellent dancers.

'At first the manager wanted the video to be based around a dance routine but I thought that might be boring. As it was their first video I knew we needed to spice it up and make it outrageous to help them make a big impact.

'The original idea was to have one close-up of a bare bottom with a piece of red jelly wobbling

around on it. We wanted to add some mystery by making people wonder whose bum it was. The bottom shot was the last one we did and it proved to be hilarious. All of a sudden all the guys started arguing about whose bum we were going to choose. In the end we decided the best thing to do was to audition them all to settle the argument. It was the end of the day and we were really tight for time so we just said, "OK, all of you get your trousers off." It was amazing. I have never seen five people strip off so quickly in my life before. They all laid down on their fronts and that made a very good shot. Gary was the most embarrassed – he started to blush and tried to cover up his bum with a towel – while Robbie was very keen.'

Ro Newton recalls how Howard was the most daring of all: 'He ended up shaking on all fours, revealing everything. We laughed ourselves silly but anticipated that it might be a bit of a problem.'

According to the producers, different versions of the video were edited, including one suitable for young fans and an X-rated version for adults. 'I was bright red and embarrassed,' says Gary. 'But the others didn't seem to have any inhibitions. They couldn't wait to get their gear off. As we showed our bums everyone from the models to the video crew just stood around looking.'

After the video shoot was over a very pleased Nigel invited everyone out for a meal at Bredbury Hall in Stockport. 'That night Gary got up and played piano in the restaurant,' remembers Angie. 'I could not believe it, he was brilliant. He played a lot of ballads, including songs by Barry Manilow and Lionel Richie – the sort of thing that would move your mother to tears. Everyone in the restaurant, from the other guests to the waiters, thought he was great. I realized there and then what a talented musician and singer he was.'

The jelly video was premiered on *The Hitman and Her* on 12 July 1991, to tie in with the release of the single.

Robbie's sister Sally remembers how the Williams family reacted when they saw the video. 'We were all shocked at first because it was very cheeky!' she admitted.

Despite the fun video and the great hopes, their first single didn't exactly take Britain by storm. It was left languishing at number 82 in the charts and the five fresh-faced guys who hoped to be the pop phenomenon of the nineties were devastated and dejected.

MAKE OR BREAK

The ups and downs of the first year

Good songs and a good stage show are not enough to get a band to the top. A group who really want to make it have to surround themselves with the right people – a dynamic manager, sympathetic record bosses and a whizz-kid record plugger to get their songs played on the radio and TV.

Another key person in the team is the press officer. Their job is a crucial one: to make sure the band get their names, faces and stories in the papers and magazines across the nation.

Take That's first press officer was Carolyn Norman. She was so convinced the band would be famous that she gave up her job to represent them!

'The band's manager, Nigel, kept saying he had this great band he wanted me to see,' recalls Carolyn. 'He thought I would be just right to work for them. When I saw them I was completely knocked out – I thought they were fantastic and had an amazing stage presence. Girls were going wild for them and it was clear to me they were going to be absolutely massive.' So she ditched in her job at Atlantic Radio to take up the challenge of turning this unknown band into the most famous teen sensation of the nineties.

Carolyn started working for Take That in April 1991, about three months before the release of the band's first single, 'Do What U Like', and through a powerful media campaign she helped transform them into teen stars.

In the early days she travelled with the band wherever they went – to clubs, radio promotions, TV appearances and even shopping centre signings. It was a non-stop gruelling schedule designed to make Take That famous – and it worked. Take That were splashed across the pages of all the teen magazines and became a name on teenage lips before they had even had a hit. 'After a while it was just wild,' says Carolyn. 'I had never seen anything like it. Wherever they went the kids would try and kiss them and grab them and hang on to their car – it was really crazy.

'The schedule was an absolute nightmare as they worked virtually every single day and night. They started off on a club tour and did as many as three or four shows a night.'

In the early days the five members of the band crammed into Gary's car or borrowed Nigel's XR3i

to get to venues. Later they took to the road in hired yellow vans, after Gary sold his car to buy a new keyboard.

Carolyn remembers the exhausting drives: 'The band couldn't afford to stay in plush hotels in those days. Instead, they would drive all the way to shows and then drive all the way back in the early hours of the morning. But the boys didn't mind. To pass the time they would have a good old singsong on those long and tiring journeys.'

Gary would often entertain the band if there was a piano around and they could always rely on Robbie to keep their spirits up and have them in stitches with his non-stop barrage of jokes and pranks. But as the band pursued fame they waved goodbye to long-term girlfriends and any normal family life. 'They worked so hard I don't think they had any time for girlfriends,' remembers Carolyn. 'I think maybe Jason and Gary had girlfriends in the beginning and I think Howard had just split up from someone. But they all realized that if they were going to make a go of it with the band they had to sacrifice having relationships.'

Song-writer Gary rarely had a moment to himself. When he wasn't performing, he was composing songs for the band's debut album. 'When the others had time off, Gary would be working, he would sit and write songs. He has this kind of quietness that allows him to just sit down and compose a love song.'

Although there was no evidence of personality clashes or rows, the band did occasionally needle Robbie. 'They picked on Robbie at one gig, saying that he hadn't got a dance step right,' remembers Carolyn, 'even though he was working really hard. But if they did have big arguments, they certainly hid it very well. I never witnessed any.'

Gradually all the hard work began to pay off and Take That started to appear in the teen magazines and even the national press. In June 1991 they featured in *My Guy*, *Jackie* and *No 1*, and in July *Smash Hits* followed suit. In August they clinched their first ever front page, in *No 1*, and *Just Seventeen* mentioned them on the cover and devoted five pages to the band inside. The Take That blitz was beginning.

'I went round to all the teen magazines and showed them pictures of the band and a video,' says Carolyn. 'It was at a difficult time because people weren't really that interested in new bands. But when they saw what they had to offer they really went for them. In the beginning we bullied and cajoled people to get them to see the band but once they did they were full of support.'

Despite the big response from the teen magazines other music biz bigwigs were not so forthcoming. They were not prepared to publicize the band until they had proof of their musical abilities – not least a Top Forty hit. Sometimes Carolyn's efforts were cruelly frustrated: 'The Radio 1 Road Show refused to feature Take That in June 1991 because they said they weren't famous enough. Nor did they support the first single, "Do What U Like". It was a blow but there was nothing we could do about it. And when we first approached the makers of the TV show *Ghost Train* they didn't think they had got what it took to appear on the show.'

At the same time as the fivesome were blitzing the media, they were constantly on the road making radio appearances and doing shows on their club tour. But things didn't always go according to plan. 'One gig we did at the very beginning for Signal Radio was quite a disaster as it had been raining and the group kept slipping and sliding all over the stage,' remembers Carolyn. 'It was very comical but not exactly the kind of impression we wanted to create. I had told the radio station that the band was going to be massive, but it was extremely hard to believe looking at the way they performed.

'About a year later Signal put them on in a local nightclub in the Stoke area and said they could have sold it out ten times over. They admitted then that I'd been right to predict the band would be massive.'

Take That also had problems at a show for Beacon Radio in Wolverhampton when the sound system broke down. 'At the time we didn't have the single cut for "Do What U Like" so we had to take a cassette to the show,' says Carolyn. 'Unfortunately they didn't have any facilities for playing the tape. There was a real panic. In the end they managed to rig up a ghetto blaster to the equipment and play the tape through that. But the music didn't come over well at all. The audience just didn't know what was going on.'

But it wasn't long before the band got their act together and began to attract crowds of wild fans who would do anything to be near them. Carolyn remembers one occasion vividly: 'At Hollywoods nightclub the girls were so desperate to see the band they smashed this plate glass window to get in. That was the kind of madness, frenzy and mayhem there was in the early days. After the show the boys had to race off in their van and they were followed by a mob of girls, who were in turn

chased by parents who were trying to catch up with them. It was bizarre.'

On one occasion a crazed fan went too far when she ripped off Mark's favourite necklace. 'Mark had a lovely crucifix on a leather string which he bought to go with all the leather gear the band were wearing at that stage. He didn't mind giving away the bandanas that he always wore, but he got upset when a fan stole his necklace as it meant a lot to him.'

In general Take That had excellent relations with their fans, as they proved to two competition winners who, thanks to *Jackie* magazine, won the chance to meet the boys – even though their parents were not entirely happy about it. 'When the band turned up in their van to pick up one girl winner, her father freaked,' admits Carolyn. 'He saw these five gorgeous-looking lads and he didn't want his daughter to go with them. In the end we managed to convince him and she went with the band to Alton Towers and had a brilliant time.'

Despite their growing legions of fans and the media coverage surrounding them, they had serious worries about whether they would ever become a chart force to be reckoned with.

After their first single bombed they had a crisis

of confidence. 'In the beginning all the record companies turned us down,' remembers Nigel. 'It was a rotten feeling and very depressing but I wouldn't be beaten. I knew the band had talent and that talent would eventually get them through.'

He was right. Interest was growing in the band as record companies became aware of just how big Take That's fan following was. Nick Raymond, head of A&R at RCA Records, decided to find out for himself what all the fuss was about. 'There was such a big buzz about them, especially from the teen magazines, that I went along to see them perform. The first show I went to was in Slough and I was really impressed by how they got the crowd on their side and won them over with their sheer enthusiasm.'

He was so impressed that he offered the band a record contract, and in September 1991 the deal was clinched. Nigel and the band were ecstatic, but there was no time to celebrate – there was work to be done.

Equipped with a record deal and a new image – they ditched the leather in favour of string vests – Take That set off on a three-week regional tour of under-eighteen clubs to promote 'Promises', their second single. Their mode of transport to and from the shows reflected their new status as a top pri-

ority for their record company. Gone were the battered cars and vans, and in their place was a flashy Renault Espace financed by the record company. They even began to taste the delights of staying in hotels, rather than driving home through the night after each gig.

When 'Promises' was released in November 1991 the band waited in suspense to see how it would do. 'The Sunday evening "Promises" made the chart we were all gathered round a radio in a hotel room, sprawled around on chairs resting our aching limbs,' remembers Jason. 'When they announced it was number 38 we all jumped on to each other and then leaped on to the bed, which we broke. Nigel cracked open the champagne, we celebrated and then went off to do a show a little bit tipsy.'

November was a bumper month for media coverage and you could hardly turn on the TV without seeing their faces on shows as diverse as *Wogan, Going Live, O-zone, Motormouth* and *Pebble Mill.* But the band's initial excitement at their Top Forty chart entry was short-lived as the single failed to move beyond number 38. Determined to do better, they put all their energies into working on their debut album over Christmas and the New Year.

But the road to fame and success was destined

to be a rocky one for Take That. The real crisis point came in January when their third single 'Once You've Tasted Love' only reached a lowly number 47 in the charts. When the band heard the news their emotions got the better of them. That night in the small and depressing bed and breakfast hotel where they were staying, they broke down and cried. Tears of frustration, tears of anger, tears of disappointment. Worse was to come the next day when RCA told them that plans to release their first album had now been put on ice.

The band's critics who had given the group a rough ride, dismissing them as brainless puppets, put the boot in further and rumours raced round the pop world that the band were set to split up. It wasn't too far removed from the truth – for Take That the future suddenly looked bleak.

'I was very worried,' admits Robbie. 'I was convinced I'd have to forget about a pop career and go back to college. It looked as if we were going nowhere.'

'We talked very seriously about splitting up around that time,' says Gary. 'If the next record had been a flop we wouldn't have been able to carry on. Though we had thousands of loyal fans, somehow we just couldn't seem to break through. We were having trouble getting our records played

on the radio and whatever we tried to do to get a big hit just didn't seem to work. But we decided not to be beaten. We knew we had something to offer. We weren't going to give up.'

The band had a crisis meeting to discuss the future and lots of problems were thrashed out. They knew they had to do something extraordinary if they were to salvage their dreams of pop stardom. Eventually they hit upon the idea of a mammoth tour of schools and youth clubs – if the fans wouldn't come to the music, then the music would come to the fans. It would mean three months of doing five or six shows a day, an incredible workload, but it was the tour that was to change their fortunes for ever.

The tour was put together in conjunction with the Family Planning Association, and was dubbed the Safe Sex tour. The Association saw it as an ideal opportunity to get across the importance of safe sex, contraception and the danger of unwanted pregnancy to thousands of schoolchildren. To the band, it was a great way to meet their fans and do something really worthwhile at the same time.

'It was great fun,' recalls Gary. 'We loaded up the car with two speakers, an amplifier, a tape deck and a microphone and went around to all the various schools that were keen for us to perform.'

They sang their songs, gave out FPA leaflets and had mini discussions with the kids about sex, AIDS, drugs, smoking – anything they wanted to talk about. 'I felt really good when the kids were asking our opinions and advice about these kinds of things,' Gary says. 'I felt as if we were helping. The kids really opened up to us and I loved that.'

The tour was a fantastic success. 'The kids were very interested in talking,' says Jason, 'and a lot of teachers came up to us afterwards and thanked us for what we had done. I think we were on their wavelength and that was why we could communicate so well.'

'Take That were very courageous to associate themselves with the Safe Sex campaign,' says Ann Furedi, former press officer with the FPA. 'I was very struck by the incredibly responsible attitude they have towards sex. They helped us a great deal by putting our message across to an audience we couldn't normally reach.'

In the meantime, the band had taken the decision to release a cover version of the Tavares classic 'It Only Takes a Minute' as their third single. Chart success was just around the corner . . .

ON THE ROAD

Take That conquer Britain

Take That were given the royal seal of approval by Princess Margaret in May 1992 when she told the band she loved their raunchy dance routines. Her Royal Highness became one of Take That's most famous fans after they attracted her attention at the Children's Royal Variety Performance which was held at London's Dominion Theatre.

When it was the band's turn to meet their first member of the Royal Family face to face they were all on their best behaviour. 'When we met the Princess she told us how much she loved our dancing and our songs,' said Jason. 'In fact she stayed talking to us for quite a while and she even cracked some jokes.'

Robbie was thrilled to meet Her Highness, who told him she loved the band's dance routines. 'She said that she was very impressed with our performance,' he reported, while Gary recalled Princess Margaret's comment on their fans in the audience: 'She said she heard all of our fans screaming for us.'

After the band's royal encounter all their months of hard slog were eventually rewarded in June when 'It Only Takes a Minute' shot into the charts at number 16 and eventually soared to number 7. It was an old soul hit from the mid seventies from American group Tavares but Take That gave it a new treatment.

'We all thought recording an oldie might do it for us,' recalls Jason. 'So we got together with stacks of records, playing our way through them, looking for the right song, and when we heard the Tavares song we knew that was exactly the right song for us.'

Take That were euphoric when they heard that the record had gone in at number 16, making it the highest chart entry since the beginning of their pop career. But even at the height of their ecstasy the band did not forget those loyal fans who had put the record in the chart. 'As soon as we heard the chart we ran out to see the fans,' says Mark. 'They were rushing around the streets outside screaming their heads off. I think they were even more excited than we were! My family were over the moon, too, but I couldn't speak to them for over an hour because my phone was busy all that

time with people ringing in to my home to congratulate me.'

Robbie was as thrilled as all the others when he heard the single's chart position. 'It was absolutely brilliant. We were over the moon, gobsmacked.'

A week after the hit single entered the charts the band were back on the promotional treadmill, appearing on a Radio 1 Road Show live from Alton Towers. Gary's mum was full of emotion as she listened to the screaming fans on the radio from her family home in Cheshire. 'Hearing those girls scream and scream, I realized that all that Gary had been working for and dreamed about all those years had been achieved. There were tears in my eyes.'

Take That had another hit single in August with 'I Found Heaven' which reached number 15 in the charts. Now – finally – the band's debut album could be released. When *Take That And Party* came out, I wrote in the *Daily Mirror*, 'It hasn't been easy for Take That to break into the big time. Now their debut album will change all that.' It wasn't a hard prediction to make. Take That were now a force to be reckoned with and the album's soaraway sales proved that. It reached number 2 in the charts, proving that Take That were here to stay.

After the album was released the band set off on their biggest yet in-store signing tour and were besieged by fans everywhere they went; 3,000 fans turned up in London, 2,000 in Glasgow and York and an incredible 5,000 in their hometown Manchester. The situation became so dangerous at the Manchester HMV store that the group had to be smuggled out disguised as policemen to stop them being mauled and hurt by the crush of hysterical fans. Four fans were rushed to hospital suffering from breathing problems, after being crushed in the crowd. In the end HMV pulled the plug on signings in Leicester, Nottingham, Reading and Croydon over fears about the safety of fans.

The band were devastated when they were forced to cancel the rest of the signings. 'Once again it's the kids who suffer,' said Gary. And he asked me to make it clear that cancelling the record store sessions was nothing to do with the band but was forced on them by the fears of the police and store bosses.

After HMV made the decision to cancel the remaining signing sessions, manager Nigel Martin-Smith fumed: 'The boys are really gutted for those fans who planned to see them and now will be bitterly disappointed. They hate letting their fans down. We think it would have been fairer to the

girls to take out more security at the other venues instead of cancelling.

'The band are very concerned for fans' safety and the last thing they want is a massive crush. As soon as they saw that the situation was getting out of control they planned their escape.'

A spokesman for HMV said: 'We felt there was a high risk that someone was going to get badly hurt so we decided to cancel the rest of their appearances at our stores.'

The panic and crush at the Manchester HMV store was just one of many scenes of Take That fan mania which followed them wherever they went. When they took to the stage at Spirals nightclub in Yate near Bristol ecstatic girls mobbed them and screamed and stamped until the band gave them an encore. After the show fans fought desperately to catch a glimpse of the boys as they followed them in convoys along motorways to their next venue.

In September Take That appealed to a wider audience with the release of a ballad, 'A Million Love Songs'. Ballads are a traditional way of attracting all kinds of listeners, especially older ones, and Take That wanted to show that they could appeal to everyone, not just the teenage fans.

It was time to tour.

*

Take That conquered Britain one cold November day in Newcastle. November 2 1992 was the date that their first major British tour started. It was also the day that transformed them into a household name.

When I went up to report on the first date of the tour for my column in the *Daily Mirror*, I went with all the enthusiasm of a pop critic about to be subjected to the latest 'teen' sensation.

I had seen teen bands come and go and, quite frankly, most of them had left me cold. Duran Duran, Wham, Jason Donovan, Bros and New Kids on the Block weren't exactly the most played records in my collection. So this afternoon when I caught the train up to Newcastle with *Mirror* photographer Chris Grieve, though not blindly prejudiced, I wasn't expecting any great shakes.

I was in for a wild surprise because that night the band were hot stuff. Though the show was carefully rehearsed and planned, I was very impressed by the group's slick singing, dancing and music.

In Wednesday's *Daily Mirror* I devoted a whole page to them.

> They may seem like an overnight success, but they are not. Take That have been slaving on songs and

dance steps for the last three years. Now all the dreams have finally come true. On Monday night they launched their sell-out British tour in Newcastle – a tour that will establish them as Britain's latest teen idols.

The group, who are currently enjoying their biggest hit, socked it to all the carping critics who said they would never make it big when they kicked off their British Tour at Newcastle City Hall. The pop world's latest teen sensation sent over 2,000 girl fans into spasms of ecstasy during their one-and-a-half hour session.

The last time a British band caused such hysteria was during the height of Brosmania. As teen idols go, they have a lot to offer. They have better songs than Bros, they are better looking than New Kids on the Block and they have more dynamism than Jason Donovan and Chesney Hawkes.

But what really sets them above their rivals is their sheer energy and enthusiasm.

They could also give Michael Jackson a run for his money when it comes to dancing. Some of their routines – which include back flips, somersaults and break-dancing – were breath-taking. They are also capable of writing good songs, as the current ballad smash 'A Million Love Songs' testifies.

They give teenage fans exactly what they want – there are plenty of suggestive hip thrusts and grinds and lots of bare flesh and rippling muscles. Before the band appeared on stage they teased the already frenzied crowd with a few bars of 'It Only Takes a Minute' and then they materialized for real, kicking off with 'Do What U Like'. By the time they finished with 'Take That and Party', not only were the group drained, physically and emotionally, but so were their audience.

After the show finished I met up with the band in the bar of the hotel where we were all staying. They were as fun and as down-to-earth as ever, incredibly polite and well-mannered. After a big show a lot of bands get delusions of grandeur – nothing excites the ego so much as an adoring audience – but if Take That's egos were big that night they certainly didn't show it.

As we talked I realized just how long they had planned and dreamed about this night. All of them had been involved in music and dancing since their early teens and all of them were perfectionists when it came to their craft. But the biggest knockout blow came when Gary revealed that he had written 'A Million Love Songs' when he was just fifteen, and he had composed dozens of other songs at that age too. I was impressed – 'A Million Love Songs' is in the same league as George

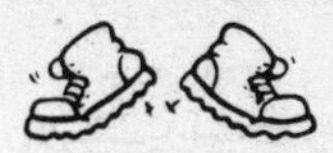

Michael's 'Careless Whisper', a pop ballad classic. Contrary to some of the publicity, I realized that the songs and stagecraft were basically all their own work. Yes, there was plenty of hype and hullabaloo surrounding them, but underneath was a bedrock of talent.

Gary revealed that the band's current smash had taken just five minutes for him to write. 'I forgot all about the song until a year later when we signed our first record contract. Most of my songs take about fifteen minutes to finish completely. I play them to my mum and gran. If they like them – we use them.'

The band fought a long hard battle to get 'A Million Love Songs' released. 'We had made our name as a dance band,' said Gary, 'and a lot of people thought that if we released "A Million Love Songs" it would be the kiss of death. But we had faith in the song and wanted it out. There were a lot of rows but in the end we got our way. And we were proved right. That song has changed our careers.'

The weeks leading up to the band's first major British tour were fraught with tension, nerves and problems. At one time Jason thought he might have to pull out of the tour after a nasty accident during rehearsals. Jason, who sported his Mohican hairstyle during the tour, pulled a hamstring during one of the group's frenzied dance routines.

'I was in absolute agony,' said Jason. 'I was rushed to see a doctor who told me to stop dancing. He said that if I carried on I could risk permanent injury. I just didn't know what to do. It was two weeks before the first show of the biggest tour we had ever embarked on and I didn't want to let them down, but at the same time I didn't want to risk damaging myself badly.

'I had to stop dancing and the doctor gave me some injections – luckily just a few days before the show everything got better and I was given the all clear.

'The day before the Newcastle show we did three rehearsals – including two full dress rehearsals. We were all so knackered – especially me. I thought my body was going to fall apart. Before the show I was actually aching all over, but once you're out there on stage in front of a screaming crowd, the adrenalin starts pumping and you forget all your aches and pains. My hamstring didn't bother me one bit. The crowd is the best doctor there is.'

As the minutes ticked away before the curtain came up on that first show, emotions got to fever pitch. Howard broke down in tears just seconds before they took the stage, as they waited to step

out in front of over 2,000 adoring fans.

'I just couldn't control myself,' he admitted. 'It was just such an emotional moment. Suddenly everything we had worked for and dreamed of was about to happen. I'm not soft, but you would have to be made out of stone not to have felt the power of that moment.'

Robbie was in the wars too: 'I had to go and see a throat specialist just before the tour started. My throat was giving me so much pain. One day it was so bad, I couldn't get to sleep at all.'

The screams that night were so loud that the next day over breakfast Gary woke up with his ears still hurting. 'I have never heard anything so loud in all my life,' he said. 'The crowd was just excellent.'

The experience of Newcastle was to be repeated over and over again on that sell-out tour as the band converted thousands of new fans to the Take That cause. Towards the end of the tour, the band came to London to play the famous Hammersmith Odeon. Afterwards they held a party at their hotel. Hundreds of Take That fans, with the kind of ingenuity that Columbo would be proud of, had found out where the band was staying and were waiting outside for them. Inside were a mass of journalists, record company workers and band friends. The Take That charm was much in evidence that night as they moved from group to group, chatting amiably away to everybody in the room.

The hard work was almost over and the boys just couldn't hide their happiness at how well everything had gone. It was obvious how much they were enjoying themselves – their smiles said it all. And it wasn't just the fans outside who were smitten by their charm. Inside, many of the women from the record company and the press – much older than the band – were bowled over by their looks and their style.

Then at 12 o'clock the band suddenly disappeared, like five Cinderellas fleeing from the ball, and the bash carried on without them. One pretty 24-year-old was crestfallen: 'That Jason is so gorgeous. I was just working up the courage to go up and ask him for a date when suddenly he and the others were whisked away.'

When they played Manchester the band could hardly contain their happiness and pride. The local lads had made it in a big way.

'That was the one when our parents turned up to see the show,' remembered Mark. 'Though they had seen us on TV and doing little personal appearances at clubs, they had never seen us do a

big show like that. It was a very special moment both for them and for us. They were all there. I remember now before we went on, we were all really nervous because that show meant so much to us. That was a really wonderful night.'

'We did two shows at Manchester's Apollo,' said Gary. 'Originally when I spoke to my mum about coming to the show, she said she would just come on the one day. But the next morning after the show she was on the phone, saying how much she had enjoyed it and that she would love to come again. That made me feel so good.'

There were all kinds of scrapes, scraps and suffering throughout their tour. In 'Give Good Feeling' there is a fight sequence and one night Robbie put his finger in Howard's nipple ring by accident and ripped it out. 'It started bleeding and it was really painful,' complained Howard.

'Howard kept kicking me in the fight sequence,' Robbie defended himself. 'And he wasn't pretending to kick me. He was doing it for real. He got really carried away.'

Mark admitted that though the dance 'fights' they do on stage are imitation, now and again things do go over the top and they end up with black eyes and cuts and bruises.

'And it's not just the band that get carried away,'

said Robbie. 'The fans watching us do too.' One of the things they throw are dummies. And a dummy travelling at full speed is like a flying bullet. 'I nearly got knocked over by one during our performance.' It's not just dummies that their adoring fans throw – there are chocolates, paper planes and cuddly toys, as well as undies and love notes.

Every town during that tour which was to change their lives for ever brought back memories. Mark has particularly fond recollections of York, the final date in the tour: 'When we started the last song of the show, "Take That and Party", the fans went mad. They began bombarding us with teddy bears. There must have been about two hundred thrown on stage that particular night. It was quite amazing. And those bears all found a good home – after each show we give all the presents to a local children's charity to help children who haven't got many toys.'

After the tour finished, the band nursed those parts of their bodies that had come in for the worst punishment: 'Our ears were really ringing and our knees were aching,' said Howard. 'After the tour I don't think my knees would have been able to take much more. They were absolutely black and blue – even though I had been using knee pads as pro-

tection the whole time. That shows just how much punishment they took.'

Gary summed things up: 'We were exhausted and knackered, but very, very happy. Performing in front of those fans was absolutely electric.'

During rehearsals, when nothing seemed to be going right, the band had got together and said a prayer. At the end of the triumphant tour they gathered in their dressing room and thanked God for their success – for Take That, there was no doubt that their prayer had been answered.

GARY BARLOW

'One day I'd like to be a pop star'

There were never any doubts that Gary Barlow would grow up to be a musician.

Born on 20 January 1971, by the tender age of thirteen the musical prodigy was already writing his own songs and performing around Britain in a band.

He was soon earning £140 a week, an incredible sum for a youngster. And by the time he was fifteen, Gary had already written some of the songs that would one day top the charts for Take That, including 'A Million Love Songs' and 'Why Can't I Wake Up With You'.

Gary was just twelve years old when he landed his first job at a club in Connah's Quay, North Wales. 'I performed at a talent show there, playing the keyboard,' says Gary. 'I didn't win, but after my performance the secretary at the club asked me if I wanted a job there! And naturally I jumped at the chance. I remember when I first went up on stage to play my songs my hands were shaking, but as soon as I touched the keyboard everything was OK.'

Gary played at the club for two years and acquired himself quite a reputation in the local area. 'I would play the organ every Saturday night for £18 an evening. It was great fun, and it was a wonderful start.'

The next musical venue for Gary was a club in the prosperous Cheshire town of Runcorn. 'In North Wales I was performing just on my own, but when I went to the club in Runcorn I had a bass player and a drummer. I considered it a move upwards,' says Gary. 'It was a very popular club and a great place for breaking new talent. Among the acts that performed there were people like Bobby Davro.

'I played there for about three years and really enjoyed it – though of course it was very far removed from the life of a pop star. I was doing cover versions while people all around me were smoking, drinking and eating chicken in a basket. But it was wonderful training – the guys in the band I was playing with were in their mid fifties, and they taught me not only a lot about music, but a lot about life, too. They were my musician years, if you like, I learned so much in them. It was while I was playing the club that I realized I wanted to

be a musician more than anything else. And I was making a lot of money too, for a schoolboy. It was as if I had struck gold.'

Throughout this time Gary was hard at work on his song-writing. 'I used to love writing songs,' he admits. 'Sometimes I would set myself the task of writing one song a day. Very often ten hours is all it would take me to write and record the whole song.' But he would very rarely draw on his own experiences for his inspiration. 'I have to say that most of my songs are written about other people's experiences and not my own – though I would never dream of telling my friends that the song is about them! When you're trying to write something from your own experience, you only get your own selfish angle. When you're looking at someone else's problems, I find that you get a much better overall view.'

He says of Take That's hit 'Why Can't I Wake Up With You': 'I wrote that back in 1987 when I was about sixteen. It was written around the same time as "Never Want to Let You Go", though it has had a few readjustments since then.'

Despite the long hours that he would devote to his musical career each week, Gary still managed to do very well at Frodsham High School. When he left the school, where his mum, Marjorie, was a teacher, he had six O levels under his belt. 'I think it was easier at school to get on with your work, than not to get on with it,' says Gary. 'If you didn't, you got hassles from the teacher – especially when your mum worked there. So I just got on with it.

'Obviously there were times when I felt really knackered – like when I had come home from a club at two in the morning and had to go to school the next day. But all in all it worked out great.'

It wasn't just Gary's mum who was aware of his prodigious musical talent, the other teachers were, too. As a young boy Gary loved to test out his compositions on the staff and students before going off to local clubs to play.

Head teacher Robin Browne recalls: 'Gary's first love was music and from a young age he had a certain star quality and stage presence. He often performed in school concerts and always appeared confident at what he did, though I imagine at times he must have felt nervous.'

While Gary was at Frodsham High School he proved he had extraordinary talent by winning two national music competitions. 'After Gary won the competitions it gave him more confidence in his musical abilities and he got a lot of good advice from the judges,' says Mr Browne. 'I'm not sur-

prised at his success but I am surprised at how quickly it has happened.'

Gary always received a lot of support from the staff and pupils. 'I remember Gary used to come and talk to me about his music, and he even gave me some of his tapes to listen to. From an early age he was serious about a music career,' says Mr Browne.

And while Gary excelled at music and put in extra hours on the piano stool he did not let his other school work suffer. 'Gary definitely stood out when it came to music but he did not let it get in the way of his school work. He was always a very popular student. And by the time he got to the fifth form he was already starting to gather fans around him, including a number of female admirers.'

Adds Mr Browne: 'He has visited the school from time to time to say hello but it has always been quite low key. I would love him to come back and perform here but I imagine it would be difficult now with all the fan hysteria.'

Gary's parents, Dad Colin and Mum Marjorie, were another constant source of support. 'They were very understanding,' says Gary. 'Of course they wanted me to do well at school, but they knew my heart was set on making music. They were great because they really let me do what I wanted to do and I am the sort of person who when they want to do something will do it. Ever since I was twelve I have directed my own life, and they never got in my way and had the utmost faith in me. I will always be grateful for that.'

But Gary's parents had some worries about the pop world, where even outstanding talent does not guarantee success or a livelihood. At one time Gary's mum wanted her son to be a policeman. 'She thought that would be a great job for Gary,' laughs the band's manager, Nigel. 'Could you just imagine him a policeman? You never know if the coppers are joking or not when they talk to you, and that's just the way Gary is.'

'My mum did want me to be a policeman,' admits Gary, 'until she got fined one day for speeding and then she cooled on the idea! I don't know why she wanted me to be a policeman. Maybe she thought I was trustworthy. Certainly I'm very strong-minded and know exactly what I want.'

Gary was the first member of the band to have purchased his own home, a pretty house in the picturesque Cheshire countryside. Gary has been able to splash out because he receives royalties every time anybody buys a copy of a record he has

written, so earns more than the other members of Take That.

'I love living out in the countryside. My house is completely detached – the nearest neighbour is around two hundred yards away,' says Gary. 'And that is nice. The life I lead is so hectic that it's good to be able to go somewhere where you can relax, far away from it all. It's very green where I am, but not too far from Manchester, so if I need to get there for something important it's no hassle. I love that area, it's where I grew up. I know a lot of pop stars live in London when they make it, but I don't fancy that. I want to stay close to my roots.

'And I don't have to travel far to work. I have built my own recording studio in my home which means whenever inspiration strikes I can put a song down on tape without too much trouble.'

Gary doesn't see why the fact that he earns more money than the rest of the band should cause problems or jealousies. 'Basically there is no difference between me and the other guys. We all have different talents. I just have a knack for song-writing. Yes, I do make more money than the others because of my writing but all the lads understand that. That's just the way it works.'

When 'Could It Be Magic', the dance version they did of Barry Manilow's 1978 hit, reached number three in the charts and became their biggest hit to date, Gary defended the band's choice to do yet another cover version: 'I don't mind doing anything, I must admit, because I'm always willing to try something new. I'm not a precious kind of song-writer. I don't think that every hit we have should be one of my own songs. I think it is good for the band to do other people's songs. Besides, cover versions are part of today's music. They introduce kids to music that they haven't heard before.

'I thought that the obvious next single off the album was "Could It Be Magic". I know record companies like new acts to do cover versions because they can often be a safe way to have a hit. I know they have talked about us doing some more and it's all right with me. So long as the records are brilliant and they're hits, I don't care what we release!'

MARK OWEN

'I prayed and prayed'

Mark Owen is the 'cutest' Take That star, say their legions of fans. He regularly sweeps pop polls in the 'Most Fanciable Male' and 'Most Kissable Lips' categories. It is not hard to see why – he has flawless skin, bright, white teeth and sky-blue eyes. Standing just 5 foot 7 inches, he is more like the fresh-faced boy next door than any of the others.

Mark, like Robbie, was a born actor, but unlike Robbie he always dreamed of a pop career. At the age of four he already had a pop idol – the most famous rock star in history – Elvis Presley. Mark's mother, Mary, has always been an avid Elvis fan – and it was a case of like mother, like son. Mark, who was born Mark Anthony Owen on 27 January 1972 in Oldham, Lancashire, says: 'I've always liked to entertain. I think that from the minute I could walk I was doing Elvis impersonations in front of the mirror. My mum had hundreds of Elvis records and she drilled her love of Elvis into me.'

Mark's sister Tracy also caught the Elvis bug.

Mark recalls: 'We used to brush our hair back, put on blue suede shoes and tight trousers, and take a tape recorder into the street outside our home where we would both do Elvis impersonations. We would put on mum's Elvis tapes and sing and dance along to them for anybody walking by. That was the first time I ever performed for anybody, but since then I've been hooked.'

At school, Oldham's St Augustine's, Mark was a member of the choir and a regular in plays. 'I always loved acting,' he says. 'I think I must have upset some of the older pupils at school because though I was younger than them I was always getting the big parts – the parts that the older guys thought they should get.' He had to put up with some teasing from his classmates, especially when his voice started to break while he was playing the role of Jesus. 'Everyone was going around taking the mickey out of me because my speeches were turning into high pitched squeals. It was so embarrassing,' admits Mark.

As well as a love for entertaining, Mark also had a talent for sport, especially football which he was completely crazy about. He was a member of a local team called Freehold Athletic and became one of their outstanding players, winning the player's player of the year award. One of his most

cherished memories of that period was scoring a hat trick during a cup final match. 'That day will stay with me for as long as I live,' says Mark, who played mainly in the midfield. 'It was like a dream come true.'

As a young teenager Mark's ambition was not to be an entertainer but to be a professional footballer. He had trials for one of Britain's greatest football clubs, Manchester United, as well as for nearby team Rochdale, but they came to nothing. Then a groin injury scuppered any chance of a career in football. 'That was one of the worst days in my life,' recalls Mark. 'I was completely shattered. I had really set my heart on becoming a professional.'

His love of sport didn't interfere with his school work and when he eventually left he had six O levels to his credit. German, Mark's worst subject, was not one of them. During one German exam he scored a measly 13 per cent, his lowest mark ever!

Mark is remembered fondly by school staff. Teacher John Fairfoull recalls him as a cheeky eleven-year-old on an adventure holiday in Tenby, and how the youngsters talked their way into entering a nightclub even though they were very under age. 'We took them out for the evening and we left them for an hour in the arcade and told them they were to meet us at the minibus. But at the allotted time there was no sign of the group. We eventually found them at the local nightclub where they had somehow managed to persuade the bouncers to let them in.'

Like the other teachers, Mr Fairfoull did not expect Mark to be a pop star. 'I don't remember him being into music while he was at school. All I do remember is that he loved football.'

That is a verdict echoed by Mark's careers teacher, Fred Laughton. 'I can't remember him showing any signs of being keen on music, singing or dancing, though I can remember his younger sister Tracy used to sing beautifully at school shows. Mark was very good at soccer though he was a little bit of a poser; he used to prepare his looks and comb his hair before and after he went on the football pitch.' It was Mr Laughton who thought Mark might have a future in banking, when Mark went to see him about his career prospects. 'Mark came to me with the idea of wanting to work in a bank and we went from there. At the time I thought it might suit him because he was a personable sort of chap and I thought he would be good with the public.'

While he was still at school Mark decided to

launch himself into the music business. He got an after school job at Manchester's Strawberry Studios where he did all kinds of tasks – including making the tea! One day he walked into the studio where Gary was recording his songs and, though they didn't know it at the time, the beginnings of Take That were born. Mark would sing the songs that Gary was writing, and the two of them decided to join forces and form a band which they called The Cutest Rush. 'The songs were good,' says Gary, 'and we made some early demos, but we never played any dates as such.'

A band can't survive on dreams alone and after Mark left school he knew he had to find work. His mum was keen for him to get a job in the bank, but for a while he worked in a trendy Oldham boutique, Zuttis. Maggie Hughes of Zuttis remembers him well. 'He got the job when he walked into the shop one day and asked if there was any kind of work. He said he was quite happy to do anything at all and he didn't mind just as long as he could earn some money. He was really nice and he had a big, beaming, bubbling smile on his face. He was always so enthusiastic, we were very taken by his personality and his manners. He didn't just impress us, he won over quite a few girls too. I remember he had lots of female admirers while he was working here. That was not only because he was so cute and good-looking but also because he was such a warm person.

'Even after he left us – and we were very sad to see him go – to work in the bank, he always came to help us out at weekends and on Sundays, whenever we needed someone. He was very obliging, a natural salesman, and people took to him because he was so pleasant. He was charming without being false. And he was a very hard worker – he always came to work before the official time and he was always prepared to stay late.

'Mark really loved music and clothes. He was always the one who put tapes on in the shop. Sometimes he would even dance to them. He was very fashion conscious. Most of the money he was paid went on buying clothes, and he always picked the trendiest stuff in our shop. He particularly liked dark colours, black and navy. He still loves clothes and enjoys trying new fashions as they come along.

'We were all thrilled when he told us he had joined Take That. It was a big thing for him to leave the safety of a secure job at the bank, but he was prepared to take that chance. I remember we made him one of the first pairs of trousers that he ever wore on stage – see-through, baggy, black

nylon – which I think he wore at a gig in Scotland. They were pretty risqué.'

The two are still good friends. 'Mark comes in the shop quite often,' says Maggie. 'A few Saturdays ago some fans arrived while he was in the changing rooms. It's lucky they didn't see him actually changing, they would have fainted. When his fans come in they leave posters, CDs and records for him to sign and he always obliges. He thinks the world of his fans. I can honestly say stardom hasn't changed him a bit. He's just as nice and normal a person as he always was.'

Mark admits that he really didn't know what job to go for when he left school. 'I worked in Zuttis, I worked as an electrician's mate and I also worked in the local Barclays Bank. I basically did bits of everything just to get some money. I did all right at school and came out with some good results but by that time I had already met Gary and I wanted desperately to do something in music. That was my real interest and I prayed and prayed that one day I would be able to do it for a living. I didn't even care if all I did at the beginning was carry Gary's equipment around. I just wanted to be part of the music world.'

His prayer was eventually to be answered – though his mum, who was so thrilled about her son getting a job in the bank, was not thrilled about him embarking on a pop career. 'Yes, my mum was wary about me becoming part of a pop group at first,' says Mark. 'But once she had a talk with Nigel and he convinced her that we did have a future, she felt much better about it. Now I think she gets more excited than most of our fans when she goes to shows. She loves the band and our music.'

Mark's success in winning the pop polls so regularly gets him a lot of playful ribbing from the other band members, who enjoy teasing each other and deflating any member's ego that gets too out of hand. 'The rest of the band call me "cute" but I don't think I am,' protests Mark. 'If I was over six foot tall they wouldn't say that about me. And maybe being cute is OK when you are young but I don't want to be called that for the rest of my life.'

It was that cuteness that resulted in the band's security being stepped up after a number of their fans said they wanted to 'kidnap' him. Mark admits: 'Some of the grownup fans quite frighten me. Especially when they get so carried away. They start off by just wanting your autograph and the next thing you know they are trying to eat half your face.'

It was Jason who turned Mark on to vegetarianism. Mark knows how important it is to keep fit and healthy in a world where you are working all hours of the day and night, seven days a week. 'I take multi vitamin tablets every single day. I find that ensures I get every supplement and vitamin I need. But I don't really like to preach about healthy eating. I'm not saying that what I take everybody should take. I think it's each to his own belief. And this is what I feel I need to keep me healthy.'

So busy is the band's schedule, Mark celebrated his last birthday in a Stockholm disco, but he didn't mind too much. 'My birthday was fun, even though it happened in a place thousands of miles away from Manchester and after a hectic day's promotion. We had a meal in a Thai restaurant and then we went to a great Stockholm hangout called Café Opera for some dancing and a little drink. But it was only a little one. Even though it was my birthday I, like the other guys, had to be in bed by twelve thirty.'

The blond-haired star, who lists his favourite bands as the Waterboys and UB 40, says that just like the rest of the band he gets incredibly starstruck when they meet up with famous pop stars. 'We are still very much in awe when we meet people. We've met Annie Lennox and Lionel Richie and I bet to a partner we were all embarrassed about asking them if it was OK to get our picture taken with them. We were all dead nervous. Meeting up with Status Quo was also great fun. I think it's important to meet other pop stars because you can learn so much from them. Status Quo have been in the business for thirty years, so they've got to be something special. They know all the ins and outs of it. What we all liked so much about them was just how friendly and down-to-earth they were. Though they have been in the business all that time and we, compared to them, are complete newcomers, they treated us with respect and that really knocked us out. They weren't at all like big shots looking down on us as just a bunch of kids. They couldn't have been warmer and more encouraging. They were really nice geezers and I'm sure that's one of the reasons they have survived in this business so long.'

Mark's musical tastes also gave the name to his pet lizard, called Nirvana after the American grunge rockers. 'I thought my lizard had died because he hadn't moved a single centimetre for hours. Then I put on a Nirvana record and he suddenly came to life. He's a great pet to have but I hope he doesn't become too much of a problem.

He's eighteen inches tall already and I have been told he will grow to over three feet.

'The other day my mum got in a real state because she thought she had killed him by spraying him with furniture polish. She usually sprays Nirvana with water but she was cleaning my bedroom at the time and picked up the wrong spray by mistake. After a few minutes the lizard, which is green, turned a ghastly shade of white and then started scuttling around the cage in a mad fit. My mum was dead upset, she thought he was about to die. Luckily the next day he had turned back to green and was in his usual dozy state.'

Mark understands that the band's hectic schedule means that sometimes friendships suffer. 'You can't really lead a normal life,' he admits. 'It's hard to see all your friends because we are away so much of the time but if they are real friends they understand all that.'

Mark, who claims one of his ambitions is to be taller, reckons he is the quietest member of the band. But when he gets on to a subject that interests him, he admits that he 'can natter on all day'. His quiet image also evaporates quickly when he does his party trick . . . when the mood takes him he leaps on to the nearest table and does those hip-grinding Elvis impersonations that he first did when he was a five-year-old boy.

Mark is sometimes teased by the other band members for being a 'mummy's boy', and while he and his mum had their fair share of disagreements when Mark decided to pursue his pop career seriously, he admits that they are very close. Like most mothers, Mary Owen had a great deal of reservations to overcome about her son getting involved with a pop group, but Mark would not be put off and repeatedly assured her that 'things would be all right'.

He got it slightly wrong. Things for Mark Owen have not only been all right, they have been awesome.

HOWARD DONALD

'I don't think I'm that handsome'

It's little wonder that Howard Donald can dance and sing so well, for performing is in his blood. Both his parents are very musical: his father was a Latin American dance teacher while his mother was a talented singer who once auditioned for the prestigious Hallé orchestra.

Howard, who is the oldest member of the group – he was born in Manchester on 28 April 1968 – definitely believes their talent has rubbed off on him. In an interview he did with me just after the band had finished their spectacular first British tour, brown-haired Howard, whose muscular frame earned him the nickname of Centrefold, admitted: 'I never knew I would be doing something like this, but I should have been prepared for it because my parents are both very musical. I guess I must have got my dancing ability from my father who earned a lot of medals for his dancing.'

Howard is the most reserved member of the group though behind his brooding good looks lies a boy who likes having fun. He admits that at school he was always the class prankster who was popular with his mates because he made them laugh. His clowning and joking could be the reason why he left school without an O level to his name. 'I wasn't too bothered about exams and that kind of thing. I preferred to make people laugh, that gave me a great buzz. I was a bit of a fool really.'

Sometimes Howard would bunk off school and spend his free time in the Lancashire countryside doing back-flips and somersaults – he excelled at acrobatics. If school could be one long gym lesson, he thought, then I could enjoy it. But school wasn't and Howard hated being cooped up in a stuffy classroom. Once he bunked off school for five weeks in a row. 'I only intended to have a few days off,' he says, 'but I kept taking another day, then another day, till the days had run into weeks. I got into awful big trouble over that.'

When Howard left school he got on to a YTS scheme, like his friend Jason Orange. Unemployment and the recession had bitten hard in the area that Howard had grown up in and he grabbed the chance of a job with open arms. He became a vehicle painter for which he earned the princely sum of £40 per week.

'It was a way of earning a little bit of money,'

remembers Howard, 'but in the end I got fed up with coming home with a face covered in red paint.'

Clubbing had always been a way for Howard to cope with the boredom of school and later the boredom of work. As a teenager he would spend a lot of nights in the local Manchester clubs, dancing to his favourite records, and the other club goers couldn't fail to notice that here was someone who could hold his own with Michael Jackson when it came to fleet-footed dance steps. Howard was already part of a break-dance troupe called the RDS Royals. One of their biggest rivals on the break circuit was a group called Street Machine, featuring a dancer called Jason Orange.

It was while break-dancing at Manchester's Apollo club that the dance paths of Howard and Jason became entwined. 'I was a regular down at the Apollo,' says Howard. 'I used to go there with a friend called Russell, and that was where I first got talking to Jason. He was in this dance crew group. We got on really well. I loved his dancing and we decided to hook up together.'

Soon Howard discovered that dancing didn't only make him feel great, it could also earn him money. He and Jason began performing their break-dance routines together and called themselves Street Beat. They were a great success and they soon found they were earning £25 a night for a show. It wasn't enough to buy a luxury mansion with, but it was a start.

Howard also found himself dancing on television, on a most unlikely programme – *Come Dancing*!

Come Dancing is a British TV institution and its mainstays are the quickstep, the waltz and the tango. In recent years, though, an offbeat section with more modern dance has been introduced and it was here that Howard found success performing an incredibly acrobatic version of some tunes from the great Hollywood musical of the fifties *Seven Brides For Seven Brothers.* The musical tells the story of a family of seven American frontiersmen who are tamed by seven beautiful women, and Howard strutted his stuff dressed in Wild West gear. His dancing and that of his team-mates went down a storm and they managed to win their section. 'I got involved with them because they saw how good at break-dancing I was and wanted something a little off the wall for the number they were going to do,' says Howard. 'And though I have always been into break-dancing, I'm also very much into choreography and love making up routines. I think that appealed to them too.'

Together with Jason, Howard is the man responsible for devising the band's sexy bump and grind routines and the one who drives the girls wild when he tears off his shirt to reveal the well-honed physique that he keeps in shape with hours of gruelling gymnastic work and a very healthy diet, usually kick-started every morning with a bowl of muesli, egg on toast and orange juice.

Howard's views can vary according to the mood he's in. Sometimes when he feels loud, he admits, 'If you've got a good body you should flaunt it,' while at other times the modest man inside him confesses: 'If a girl says I have a nice body, I go quite shy. I don't think I'm that handsome.'

The pranks and hoaxes that he perfected at school have now found their way into the band's life and they liven up the days when the pressures of their success, as well as their gruelling work schedules, threaten to get the better of the boys. One piece of mischief that is talked of to this day is the time Howard laced Mark's codpiece with itching powder. 'I have never seen anyone dance so fast in all my life. Not even Michael Jackson,' laughs Howard, who votes Michael Jackson as the superstar he would most like to meet.

Though he is often shy and modest in interviews, one topic that is guaranteed to get Howard fired up is the comparison of the band to American teen idols New Kids on the Block. The New Kids dominated the pop world in the late eighties, enjoying a string of hits all over the world. There are many comparisons for the critics to latch on to: both bands have five good-looking guys in them, both bands feature breath-taking dance skills and both bands drive female fans crazy with their romantic songs, stunning looks and 'strip' routines. Howard got sick of hearing about the New Kids at a very early stage: 'All those comparisons are ridiculous. If you saw us on stage, you would see the difference. Our routines are much tighter and much more varied.' He also reacted strongly to suggestions that the band were cynically manufactured and hyped. 'People who say that don't really know what we're about. We write more of our own material and we do our own choreography. We're in control when it comes to our music and our look. We always want to keep our ideas and songs fresh – that's important for us if we want to keep moving ahead.'

When Howard was offered the job in Take That his mum, like most of the other parents, was concerned. 'She was worried it was just a pipe dream that would never amount to anything,' says Howard. 'I felt a bit bad at first, too, because when

I was doing my vehicle painting job I was giving Mum a regular amount of money every week. When the band started I did a few odd jobs but they didn't bring in enough money to be able to pay for my keep. So I was basically giving mum nothing.' To his relief, this isn't a problem he has to worry about any more.

Howard has suffered a series of injuries thanks to the band's exhilarating, often dangerous, dance routines. On one occasion the dance steps were so hot they burnt his feet – literally! 'We were doing a summer road show and like an idiot I decided to take my shoes off. What I hadn't reckoned with was that we were dancing on a metallic floor which got hotter and hotter as the sun beat down on it. I didn't feel any pain because I was so engrossed with what I was doing, but at the end of the show I was in real pain. The soles of my feet were burnt and covered with blisters.' But potentially his most lethal accident happened before the band was formed when he was involved in a car crash. 'I had only been driving for about six months,' recalls Howard. 'I was on a dual carriageway with a friend and it was pouring with rain. All of a sudden, two of the cars in front of me slowed down and I slammed on my brakes to avoid hitting them. It didn't work. Because it was so wet I skidded completely out of control and smashed into the car in front, while my back end hit another car. I caused a five-car pile-up. All these women got out of the cars sobbing their eyes out. I couldn't believe what had happened. I sat in my car, paralysed, not knowing what to say or what to do. It was a nightmare. But, thank God, miraculously no one was hurt.'

Howard, who like Mark and Robbie still lives at home, understands why groups turn to drugs. 'I think one of the reasons is because there is so much pressure and so much work. Groups think drugs might help them cope. But it's a false belief. In the end they wreck your life. We have never taken them and we never would.'

Out of all the Take That members, Howard is the one who has the most trouble getting up in the morning. He says: 'I remember when I used to have to be somewhere in the morning by eight thirty, I would never wake up until eight thirty. I can't help it, I love my bed.'

The band's manager has invented his own ruse to solve Howard's sleepyheadedness. Says Nigel: 'Whenever they are staying overnight at a hotel, I will always put a phone call down to reception to ask what time Howard has booked his wake-up call for. It is always about one-and-a-half hours

later than the rest of the band, so I tell them to make sure they wake him up one-and-a-half hours earlier than he wants. It's the only way we can get him out of bed.'

JASON ORANGE

'I wanted to be a dancer'

Jason Orange owes his big break to a friend's girlfriend. She realized what a fantastic dancer he was and decided that his talent shouldn't be hidden from the world.

One night after watching Jason and his best friend Neil McCartney holding court on the dance floor of a local Manchester club, she wrote a letter to the TV programme *The Hitman and Her* telling them all about him. Jason knew nothing about it till he received a note from the show asking him to come and try out for an audition, but soon he was showing his fancy footwork in front of the millions who watched the programme every Saturday night.

Jason says: 'I owe her so much thanks for that. She used to come and watch us dance all the time and thought we were brilliant. She would get dead excited about the routines we did. She was a big fan of the *Hitman* show and one day she decided to write to them.

'When I got the letter from them asking us to come up for an audition it was like a bolt out of the blue. But I knew it was a wonderful chance. I was very nervous about the audition but we did fine and they asked us to be on the programme. Those were great days. I had a lot of fun.'

Jason comes from a big family, whose parents divorced when he was young. He has an identical twin brother, Justin, an older brother, Simon, three younger brothers, Dominic, Sam and Oliver, and two half-sisters. His mother works in a doctor's surgery and his father is a bus driver. At school he was shy and retiring. 'I never joined in class discussions or put forward my point of view,' he admits. 'It was as if I was enclosed in a kind of shell.'

Jason's twin brother Justin was born just twenty minutes after him. The two of them have an incredible communication, which sometimes borders on the psychic. When they were growing up they would laugh and cry at the same kind of things, and often intuitively knew what the other was doing, even if they were miles apart. They looked incredibly like each other – before Jason grew his goatee beard – which resulted in them always getting mistaken for each other.

Their identical looks got Jason into plenty of

trouble during his teenage years from jealous boyfriends. 'Girlwise he was ahead of me,' remembers Jason. 'He used to chat up or romance other guys' girlfriends and they would come up after me or give me a beating because they thought I was him.'

Jason was not a brilliant scholar and, like Howard, with whom he does the band's choreography, he lived for dancing. He would spend as much of his spare time as he could dreaming up new routines in the Manchester clubs for his dance group the Street Machine.

When he left school, also like Howard, he joined a YTS scheme and trained as a painter and decorator. 'I worked for the local Manchester council, for their Direct Works Department,' said Jason. 'For some reason they decided to take me on to do a full apprenticeship and I worked there for about four years. I was pretty lucky to have a job, because a lot of my friends just couldn't get one, no matter how much they tried. Times were tough. I enjoyed a lot of the work. One of the things I liked about it was that it was a trade and I realized that it was very important to get a good trade behind you. Something that you could always use.'

Jason mainly painted council houses, both the inside and the outside, though more often than not he ended up outside: 'They used to throw me outside all the time because I was a cheeky git to the foreman. Standing outside in the freezing cold in the winter to burn all the paint off the window-sills was one of the worst jobs you could ever do, and it was their way of pushing people. I used to get that all the time.'

Despite his cheek, the other workers liked Jason and Jason liked the job. There were a lot of fun moments and a lot of mishaps too. 'I've dropped a few pots of paint on a few floors, and fallen off a few ladders too,' remembers Jason. 'The worst accident I was involved in was one where I very nearly burned a house down. I had been asked to burn the paint off a door of a shed in a yard. When it got to brew time, I left all the gear in the shed and went off with the other guys for a cup of tea. When I got back I opened the door and the shed was on fire! I don't know how it happened. Luckily there was nothing inflammable in the shed and I desperately ran around looking for water to put the fire out. I felt like a right plonker, though I managed to put the fire out quite quickly. But it could have been nasty. If I had spent a little longer drinking tea, the house could well have burned down.'

While working as a painter and decorator, Jason spent more and more time dancing. His first dance

partner was Neil McCartney, who was part of the break-dancing troupe, Street Machine. He had also met up with Howard Donald in a local Manchester club and worked out a few routines with him.

It was while Jason and Neil were dancing on *The Hitman and Her* that their paths first crossed with that of Nigel Martin-Smith. At that time, Nigel was dreaming about forming the perfect teenage band. He had already sized up Gary Barlow and was now looking for four other guys. At first Jason just wasn't interested in Nigel's plan. Nigel recalls the occasion: 'I was down at the *Hitman* on the show with another act of mine, Damien, who was enjoying a big hit with "Timewarp", a number from the *Rocky Horror Music Show*. Jason's friend Neil approached me and told me they were looking for a manager. I wasn't really interested in Neil but I was in Jason. I thought he had a lot of star quality. But it was funny because Jason didn't really want to know about being in a pop group. He was quite happy being a dancer and wasn't bothered about anything else. I couldn't believe how dead cool he was.'

Jason himself adds: 'I was young then, young and daft. I was enjoying myself. And I just wanted to carry on enjoying myself.'

Nevertheless, Nigel eventually managed to convince Jason that his brilliant dancing could be an essential ingredient in the group he was forming. Though many of the mums were wary for their boys, Jason's mum wasn't – she was happy for Jason to join the band. As we sit talking in a plush boardroom on the sixth floor of their record company's office in Putney, Southwest London, Jason says: 'My mum was happy with anything I wanted to do. She was cool. She wouldn't mind if I was on the dole as long as I was happy. She's very young minded and believes life should be about happiness and enjoyment.'

The other band members like Jason's mum, too. She could easily pass for his older sister and all the band members joke about fancying her. Says Mark: 'His mum is very young. When Jason had his picture taken alongside her she looked just like his girlfriend. All the lads think she's a bit of all right.'

Jason, quite astounded by their reaction, manages to say: 'I wish my mum could hear all the lads speaking about her like this. It would make her day.'

Although Jason's mum was keen on him joining a pop band, Jason still had serious reservations. For one thing he had a steady job in a good trade and was earning a regular wage. He sought the

advice of Peter Wilson, the personnel officer at Manchester City Council Direct Works Department, before he decided to give up his job. 'Jason came to talk to me several times about whether he should leave the department or not when the opportunity arose for him to join the band,' remembers Mr Wilson. 'He was concerned that he was giving up a secure job and he knew he was taking a risk. I asked him if he had looked into everything and if he could see a future with the band and he said there was a good chance they would be a success.

'When he eventually decided to leave he was very excited and told us all to watch out for Take That. He was dead right.'

Jason had some qualms about actually passing an early audition for the band because 'before then I had only ever sung in the bath'. But he got through and quickly became a key member of Take That. He is the second oldest member of the group, born on 10 July 1970, and is the most grown-up looking with his Mohican haircut and goatee beard. Life with the band has changed his personality dramatically from the shy youngster he was at school. 'Though I do have a shy and sensitive side, these days I'm a bit of an exhibitionist. I like to be up front and speak for the band.' The other members say he is a great laugh, but they also point out what a perfectionist he is and how fastidious he can be. It is true. Jason insists on practising a dance routine till every step is absolutely perfect.

'I was totally different a year ago to what I am now,' admits Jason. 'And I know that in the next few years I am going to change more and more. Being in a band like this just can't help but change you. You meet so many people, see so many things – you can't help but learn and be influenced by everything around you.'

Jason is also the most health conscious member of the band. His diet consists of plenty of fresh fruit and vegetable juices. 'I believe that you should look after your body and because of that it's important what you put into it. I like to eat fresh food, food which is packed with vitamins. I also make sure I take plenty of cod liver oil and yeast tablets. And I have a daily drink of raw vegetable juice. It's made out of carrot, beetroot, cabbage and several other kinds of vegetables. Robbie says it smells and tastes horrible, but I love it. It does me the power of good.'

ROBBIE WILLIAMS

'I was always a bit of a joker'

Unlike the other members of Take That, Robbie Williams had no desire to be a pop star. Take That's youngest member always had a burning ambition to be an actor. From his childhood days, dark-haired, steel grey-eyed Robbie had been crazy about the movies.

His idols were movie stars, the distinguished and debonair star Cary Grant and Cockney actor Michael Caine. It was the thought of becoming a star just like them that had driven Robbie to Nigel Martin-Smith's agency in the hope of some acting work.

But Nigel had other plans for him. When he realized there was a certain something missing from the group he was putting together, he drafted Robbie in as the fifth member.

It was an irony which was not lost on the star, for when he was growing up his mum always asked him if he would like to be a pop star, the dream of so many other little boys, and Robbie always answered her 'No'. Robbie, known as the baby of the group – he was born on 13 February 1974 – told me: 'I remember very clearly watching TV when I was really young and Kajagoogoo coming on. My mum turned round to me and said, "I bet you would like to be a pop star just like them." She was quite taken aback when I told her that being a pop star didn't interest me at all, and that what I wanted to be more than anything else was an actor.'

Robbie's dream was not idle talk. 'I was entering talent competitions from the age of four or five,' he says, 'and acting from about seven years old.' But acting is one of the toughest professions to break into – as tough as pop music – and young Robbie found the going difficult at first. 'I just used to go to as many auditions as I could. At first I had no luck at all. I would get rejected for all kinds of reasons – either I was too small, too tall or the wrong shape. But I refused to be beaten. And in the end I found myself up there acting on stage. At that time I was doing dramas or musicals in local theatres close to where I lived. But it was wonderful. I adored what I was doing.'

Among the local shows that Robbie appeared in was the Hollywood musical *Chitty Chitty Bang Bang* and Charles Dickens' classic story of an

orphan boy in Victorian England, *Oliver Twist.*

In *Oliver Twist* Robbie played the part of the Artful Dodger, a streetwise teenager who is Fagin's most accomplished pickpocket and who befriends Oliver Twist when the youngster joins Fagin's den of thieves. 'That's a part that a lot of stars do when they are children,' says Robbie. 'Phil Collins is just one of the people who have been the Artful Dodger during their career. It's a great part to play. I had a constant big cheeky grin on my face and my hair kept falling into my eyes. It was really long and the production people wouldn't let me get it cut. I know there are pictures of me as the Artful Dodger floating around. I think I looked pretty yucky, it would be awful if those pictures surfaced.' He also had a minor appearance in one of television's best loved soap operas, *Brookside.* So Robbie's acting career was showing definite signs of promise when fate took a different turn.

Nigel Martin-Smith had Robbie in mind as the fifth member of Take That, but first Robbie had to have yet another audition. This one was to prove the most important audition of his life. 'I sang a Jason Donovan hit, "Nothing Can Divide Us", for the audition,' says Robbie. 'I must have been OK because all the guys agreed that I should be in the band.'

Show business has always been in Robbie's blood. His dad is comedian Pete Conway, who once won the top television talent show *New Faces*, and his mum, now separated from his father, comes from a musical family. 'When our families used to get together at Christmas time or other holidays there were always singalongs and charades,' says Robbie. 'It was great fun.'

Brought up in the potteries town of Stoke-on-Trent, Robbie left St Margaret's Ward School with only two exam passes. He says of his childhood: 'My parents split up when I was young and I lived with my mum. I was always a bit of a joker at school and I guess that's why I didn't get any good exam results. I found out very early on in my schooldays that one of the keys to being popular was making the other kids laugh. So that's what I did. I was just this chubby boy who would go around pulling faces and telling jokes and I found myself with a big circle of friends.'

Robbie was known as the class joker and his pranks have passed into school legend. Teachers at St Margaret's remember him with affection. Head teacher Conrad Bannon says: 'Robbie was bright, lively and always had a smile on his face. He was the life and soul of his class. He was very popular both with his classmates and with members of

staff. He wasn't shy at all, he was a real extrovert. His great love was acting and he was always performing in various school plays and productions. He also did lots of acting in local theatres.

'We are the best school in the county for music and every child who comes here has to learn a musical instrument. Robbie would have been in very musical surroundings. But I never thought he would become as famous as he is now. I never thought that was his aim in life.'

Deputy Head John Thompson remembers Robbie as a joker, but says, 'There was never any malice in the jokes he played. He liked to have fun, but he always knew where to draw the line. He livened up class lessons but never in any negative way.

'One of my strongest recollections of Robbie was when a number of children went to a Catholic retreat centre called Soli House in Stratford-on-Avon. All the children were discussing moral issues, such as poverty, and each group had to put on a little production to examine the various issues. Robbie always led everyone in the discussions and was the one who really helped organize the playlets. He was good at adlibbing and he thought very quickly.'

Robbie's athleticism in dancing showed itself

early on during his schooldays. He loved most sports, especially football, and he is an avid Port Vale supporter. He also enjoyed cricket, though it was cricket that nearly caused him to have a fatal accident while he was on holiday as a youngster. 'I was in Salisbury in South Africa where I was playing at a local cricket club,' recounts Robbie. 'I ran into the outfield to retrieve a ball that had been hit there and as I put my hand into the long grass I heard this loud hissing noise. I looked down and there was this big snake nestling by the ball. I was petrified. Afterwards, when I told the other guys in the cricket team what had happened and described the snake, they told me how poisonous it was, and how I had been lucky to get away without being bitten.'

Just like Jason and Howard, the break-dancing bug hit Robbie, too, while he was still at school. 'He always loved dancing as a child,' recalls a friend. 'Almost every Saturday for months Robbie and a gang of schoolfriends used to go break-dancing outside Potteries shopping centre in Hanley.'

Robbie has lots of different musical tastes but – like the rest of the band – he greatly admires the Pet Shop Boys, Neil Tennant and Chris Lowe. 'They were the pop stars I most wanted to meet,'

▲ The Best Band in the World – Ever! The boys sweep the board at the 1993 *Smash Hits* Awards

Gary shares a drink with manager and mentor Nigel Martin-Smith ▼

▲ The White Stuff!

New Dos - Robbie displays his shocking new hairstyle, while Howard's new look is *dread*ful! ▼

▲ Right By Your Side: Mark and Jason arrive at the Take That party with the ever-present security guards to protect them

All smiles, but Robbie was growing tired of Take That's lack of freedom and all-work-and-no-play schedule ►

◄ Bod God – Howard gets in trim while Jason prefers a more relaxing way of getting about – and takes his rubbish with him! ▼

Love and Peace – Robbie gets festival fever at Glastonbury ►

◄ Robbie's blackened tooth may be false but his Glastonbury frolics earned him a black mark in the Take That camp

▲ And Then There Were Four – Take That's first appearance on Top of the Pops without Robbie

'Never Forget' sings Mark, but will he forget his best mate Robbie? ▼

▲ Flashy Foursome – the new-look Take That arrive at the National TV awards

Going Solo - Robbie arrives alone and keeps his mouth closed about the split ▶

◄ Robbie reveals all – and has the girls flocking! ▼

says Robbie. 'I just couldn't believe it when they turned up to one of our shows. It was so brilliant talking to them. Their music is excellent. Simple pop music, but so brilliant.'

Another fave is soul singer Lionel Richie, who writes some of pop's most romantic songs, including 'Hello' and 'Dancing on the Ceiling'. 'I just love the sentiments in his songs. It makes me laugh when people say he has had his day. His Greatest Hits album just wouldn't stop selling. He will be going for years.'

Robbie's mum was the most reluctant of all the band's mothers to let her son join Take That because when he auditioned he was so young. 'I was in the fifth year at school when I auditioned for Nigel,' says Robbie. 'My mum wanted very much for me to go to college. I would have liked to go and do English and drama at sixth form college and then eventually go to university to read drama. I had dreams of being a drama teacher.'

But it was a dream that was never to be because Robbie passed his audition to become the fifth member of Take That. 'It's a day I will never forget. Not only because it was the start of a new life for me but also because looking back on it now, it was so hilarious. It was the day that I got my exam results. I went down with my friend Lee to find out how I had done and I remember how we were both petrified about opening the envelopes that contained our academic futures. What made it even worse was that everyone around us was shrieking with delight at how they had got eight O levels or nine GCSEs. All the time Lee and I were just looking at each other, not daring to open the envelope, especially now that so many of our other schoolmates were so chuffed by the results. In the end we plucked up the courage to find out how we had done. We opened them nervously and saw we both only had two passes each. We decided to drown our sorrows, went down to the off-licence, got some drinks and just sat there wondering what we were going to do with our lives – whether we should join the Foreign Legion or what.

'I had almost forgotten all about my Take That audition. I had done it about a month before and hadn't heard anything. So I was blown away when I finally arrived home and my mum said she had some good news for me. She told me Nigel had been on the phone and that I was in the group. I couldn't believe it. I felt so ecstatic. It was such an amazing turn around to the day. So Lee, me and a couple of other mates went down the offy again – this time not to commiserate but to celebrate.'

It was Robbie, the tallest member of the group at six feet one inch, who invented one of Take That's most distinctive images, the dummy. After fans saw Robbie wearing a dummy in one of the band's photographs, thousands of them followed suit and now their concerts are awash with a sea of dummies. But it was Robbie's dummy that was to worry many people who were concerned that the energetic singer might be on drugs. He was besieged by hundreds of letters from fans who were terrified that his habit of sucking dummies was evidence that he took the rave drug Ecstasy – Ecstasy users often stuff dummies in their mouths while out clubbing because the drug makes them want to chew.

In the end, Robbie asked me if I could put a message out through my *Daily Mirror* pop column, reassuring fans that he wasn't an Ecstasy user and that there was absolutely no cause for concern. He told them: 'Please don't fret. I'm not on drugs. It's just an image, I think it looks good.

'I have had a lot of frantic letters from fans who are worried that I am hooked on drugs,' admitted Robbie. 'I want to set their minds at rest. I don't take drugs and have no interest in them at all. We are a clean-living group. I know that dummies are connected with the Ecstasy scene but that's not why I have them. The story behind my dummy couldn't be more innocent. A terrible spot came up near my mouth just a few hours before I was due to do a photo shoot with the rest of the guys. I hit upon the idea of sticking a dummy in my mouth to conceal it.'

During that interview Robbie was very concerned that innocent Take That fans could find themselves under suspicion from the police because they carry dummies. 'When I went home recently I found out that the police had confiscated a lot of dummies from our fans. I meet a lot of the local girls and boys, I love chatting with them and finding out what's been happening at home. I couldn't believe it when they told me that the police had been down to where they hang out and confiscated all their dummies. They said what they were doing was drug-related. Apparently they've been doing that up and down the country.

'I was also told that the police have been going into schools and giving talks about dummies. I was told that they were telling kids that sucking a dummy can give you a buzz, but it can also dehydrate you. That's nonsense. What is upsetting is that the police could be linking me with a drug craze. And it's just not true.'

NIGEL MARTIN-SMITH

'It's a dream come true'

He could easily be mistaken for one of the group. He has short blond hair, lively blue eyes and wears the latest fashions. He is Nigel Martin-Smith and everywhere Take That go, he goes too.

But he is not Take That's secret sixth member, he is the Svengali behind them – the band's manager. He planned and plotted, schemed and sweated to create a teenage band that could take on the world. And now his dream has come true. Nigel, who owns a Manchester-based talent agency, spent years trying to get his band together. The idea for it was there two long years before Take That was formed and the idea initially came about because of a rival band – New Kids on the Block.

During the eighties the New Kids, a five-piece outfit from Boston, USA, were the biggest teen sensation in the world. Their faces were plastered all over bedroom walls from New Zealand to Norway, and their record sales were staggering. Nigel

Martin-Smith bumped into them during the making of a TV show in Britain. He was impressed by their music – a mix of rap and dance – but not by them. 'It must have been one of the first TV shows that the New Kids had done in this country,' recalls Nigel, 'and I couldn't help but feel how obnoxious they were. They seemed to be very big-headed, strutting around the studio as if they owned it.

'It had always been my obsession to put together a band of unemployed lads, make them into a group and break them. I got fed up with always seeing bands from America or from London making it and I wanted to create a Northern group. The day I saw New Kids on the Block it all suddenly gelled. There was a huge fuss over the New Kids but I was sure I could form a band which could create an equally big stir but be charming, friendly and down-to-earth at the same time. I didn't think it would be hard to find a group of talented youngsters because having an agency I knew just how much talent there was out there. What I wanted to get right was to find five guys who were all likable and not big-headed. I would like to think I have succeeded. The only part of my dream that I got wrong was the bit about "unemployed" kids – this lot were all employed!'

The band was built around the foundation block of Gary Barlow, the first member that Nigel signed to a management deal. 'Gary had an incredible amount of writing talent,' says Nigel. 'At first I took him on as a solo artist, but I realized that he would be best in a band because his interest at the time was more in the studio than anything else. I knew Mark, too, because he hung around with Gary a lot. Then Jason and Howard turned up on the scene and before I knew it I had the band that I had always dreamed of, right there smack bang in front of me.'

But there was one thing missing – a fifth member of Take That. Nigel Martin-Smith decided he needed another member as a safety measure: 'The reason I insisted on getting another member was because I thought to myself that it could be a year or two before they got off the ground – and in that time, anything could happen. Especially one member deciding to leave, which could weaken the group.

'That was the real reason, at first, that I put Robbie in. I thought that one or two of them might drop out because it takes a lot of time to make it in this business and in my experience many people do not stay the course. They leave for all kinds of reasons – because they don't like the struggle, their parents want them to get a proper job or they're disillusioned. I didn't want any of that. I wanted the band I created to survive.'

Robbie Williams was picked out as a potential fifth member for the group and was made to audition. 'I wanted to make sure we got the right guy,' says Nigel, 'so I picked the Jason Donovan song "Nothing Can Divide Us", which is one of the hardest songs in pop to sing. I did that on purpose. Robbie was quite a good singer and I wanted to see how far I could stretch him.' Of course, he came through with flying colours.

All the band have different looks, style and personality. But though much around the band was calculated and carefully planned, their image was not. 'No,' says Nigel, 'that is just a natural thing. They are all very different guys and I encouraged them to have and develop their own personalities. I didn't want them all to be clones.'

One of Nigel's hardest tasks was to persuade all the parents to let their sons pursue a pop career. When the band actually signed their contract, Nigel invited most of the parents to be there, to check that nothing underhand was happening. Says Nigel: 'The toughest mum for me was Robbie's mum because Robbie was still at school. He was a bit of a baby when he auditioned for

the band. His mum is a businesswoman and quite astute. And when she came in to meet me, she fired twenty questions at me about the plan I had, the way I was going to work and the future of the band. She was the one who gave me the hardest time.'

Many of the mums were wary – but what helped convince them in the end was money. Not the money that their sons might or might not earn, but the money that Nigel was ploughing into the band. 'I remember I got all the mums together and spelt it out to them. I said – I know you are worried about this, but I have put £80,000 into this band so believe me I am just as worried. When they found out how much I had invested, they realized I meant business.'

The difficulty Nigel experienced with getting the group signed up to a record company has left him with harsh feelings about a lot of the music business. He believes many record companies aren't interested in giving the public what they want, but instead what they think the public should have. 'Too many people in the music business are worried about signing acts that are credible,' says Nigel. 'They sign up prestigious acts that their mates will approve of. So much of the music industry is pretentious. It's a real joke. That's why when people like myself and Pete Waterman come along, who believe in giving the public what they want, we rock the boat. It's the same with rave music. That is being bought in droves by kids on the street, but most of the record companies look down their nose at it because they don't think it's "musical" enough.'

Though Nigel may look like one of the band members' older brother, he acts like their father. He is loving and considerate, but also strict. He makes the rules and the band have to play by them. Most nights the lads have to be tucked up in bed by 12.30. It is one of many tough rules that Nigel has imposed, and a hard one to accept when you're 22 years old and see the world as your oyster – but it is there for a reason. 'Nigel believes in working hard,' says a friend of the band, 'and though the band is fun, this is not a game. There is an awful lot at stake. Every day there is so much to do, and he always wants the band to be at their freshest.'

The rules don't just ensure the band devote themselves totally to their career, they are also designed to keep them down-to-earth. 'At one point,' adds the friend, 'Nigel insisted that the band do all their own housework and wash all their own clothes. More than anything he wants to

prevent them from getting spoilt, big-headed and developing huge egos. He wants to make sure that their feet stay firmly on the ground.'

TRUE LOVE

Take That and romance

Take That will not be able to fall in love for two years . . . on their manager's orders. And that's bad news for the millions of girl fans the band have all around the world.

The band can have flings and flirtations, but anything steady is banned by Nigel Martin-Smith. And strict and harsh as it seems, the band have agreed to say no to love for that period. The reason love is a no-go area is because the band's shrewd though charming manager believes it could be the downfall of their career. Once a band member falls in love, his girlfriend could start to mean more to him than the band, worries Nigel. He knows that separating boys from true love is as difficult a task as separating cornflakes from milk, but he is determined to succeed.

Nigel is also worried that if one of the lads falls in love and has a steady relationship, he will no longer find himself so popular with the fans and that could be damaging to the band. When it was erroneously reported that Take That had a candlelit dinner with the five-piece all-girl Aussie band Girlfriend, there was panic in the Take That camp. The item said that the two groups had met in a German hotel and they had all taken a shine to each other. The band's press officer Loretta de Souza rang me up to ask me to put an item in my *Daily Mirror* column denying that the groups were romantically linked.

There was no truth in the story and I was more than happy to say so:

> Take That are completely baffled by a report that they have been out on candlelit dinner dates with Aussie all-girl fivesome Girlfriend. Says Gary Barlow, whose new single 'Why Can't I Wake Up With You', is released next month, 'It's rubbish. We were at the same hotel as they were, but we weren't even sitting at the same table. Someone obviously has a lively imagination.'

After the band got back from their promotional tour, Gary again brought the subject up in an interview. 'I was really upset about that,' he told me. 'We are with the same record company as Girlfriend in Germany and they and some of Girlfriend's people came up with the idea. They thought it was good publicity. We didn't mind

meeting them as they were staying in the same hotel but when we turned up there were two photographers and we were told they wanted us to sit next to a girl each. We didn't agree to it at all. There was no way we were going to do something like that. They wanted to get some publicity by using us. It happens all the time.'

Nigel has plenty to say on the subject of girls: 'Yes, I have stopped the boys from having steady girlfriends for about two years. It has caused a lot of rumours, with some people saying it's not natural for guys of their age not to have regular girlfriends, while other people are saying they must be gay, but I stand by what I did. I have never insisted they behave like monks, but what I don't want is for them to get involved in heavy, serious relationships because there is just no room in their lives for that. They are away from home all the time now because of the pressures of their pop success and if they had a relationship that would be so hard for them to deal with. They wouldn't want to leave home and leave their girlfriends. Romance is a very powerful force and if they had serious relationships that could and most probably would become the number-one thing in their lives.'

He warned the band about the 'no girlfriends'

rule right at the very beginning. 'I told the band – if you do everything I tell you right from the start, this is exactly the way your career will go – and I showed them the plan for their future. But I believed that plan could only work if they put their serious love life on hold for two or three years. I told them that once they had really made it and they had got to a certain level then they would be able to do what they wanted. But I spelled it out to them that if they wanted a career they had to work damn hard for the next three years and give up any thoughts of a serious romance, and to be fair to them that's what they've done.

'Right from the word "go", no girlfriends or friends have ever been able to come to the shows and if they want their family to come, they have to ask me first. That just ensures that everything is kept on a very professional level.

'There's a lot of trust between me and the band and that's the way it has got to be. I've always been very open with them and they've always been very open with me – that's the way it has always worked. Everything we do is discussed in the band meetings we have each week. That's when we all sit down and I ask them if they have got anything to moan about, and they moan and tell me the things that are going wrong or the things they are

not happy with and we try to sort things out. Because we discuss everything, they are just as involved in the management decisions as I am. That's the kind of relationship it has to be.'

But the real worry for those around Take That is whether the boys will be able to do without love for two years. The band believe they can and say they will stick to Nigel Martin-Smith's order.

It will be harder for some than others. The band member Nigel most worries about is Howard Donald. Howard loves the comfort, warmth and security that a steady relationship can provide and Nigel believes he is the one member who will most miss a steady girlfriend. 'Howard really needs a relationship. He's going mad because he needs to be with somebody but he knows that he can't.'

Howard himself admits it. 'That's true and that's why I can see that the rule about no girlfriends makes sense. Once I fall in love, I fall in love very deeply and I think that to be in a relationship like that and to spend so much time away from a girl would be unbearable and unfair for both of us. But the way things are now, if I was to meet the right girl I would never find out if she was the right one because I wouldn't be able to spend enough time with her.'

Gary has similar views: 'Nigel isn't forcing us

into anything. He has just made us see the sense of the fact that if we want careers we have got to keep our minds on the job. We will all have relationships one day, we know that. But even when we decide that the time is right, it won't be easy because we will be in a position where a girl could easily like us because of what we are rather than who we are. I would like to think that we are all level-headed and smart enough to see through a girl who might just want to go out with us because we are rich and famous.'

But even Gary has to admit how much he likes steady relationships and how he looks forward to marriage one day. 'I have had two main steady girlfriends,' he reveals. 'The last one was a girl called Nicky, we had been going out for about three years. I did like having steady relationships but you have to face up to the fact that they don't always last.

'I know that my first relationship ended when I came to an age where I had outgrown it. The second one broke up mainly, I think, because I was moving into a totally new life. I was starting to write songs with Mark and then we did the *Hitman* TV shows and things started to happen. I went off on another wavelength and that was that really. I see girls when I go back home all the time, but

never anybody steady. I know how demanding that would be, especially with the kind of work we are doing at the moment.

'But I do eventually want to get married and have kids. I don't want the business to interfere with those plans, because I don't want to miss out too much on what I want to do in life – and that can happen when the business takes over and you are under all kinds of pressure.'

Mark Owen is the band member who rates highest with fans on the cute-o-meter. He has always been a magnet for girls. Now, though, the adulation is of the kind most men could only dream about.

He too has had a steady girlfriend, but now says, 'It would be impossible for me to keep a regular girlfriend happy and be in the band at the same time. There would be too much pressure. Your girlfriend would be upset by the fact that you just never got to see her enough, as well as getting jealous of other girl fans. I prefer to be on my own or chill out.

'You have to take it one step at a time. It would be difficult to concentrate on your music and your band – and have a girlfriend at home at the same time.'

Occasionally the lack of a regular girlfriend can cause problems, finds Mark. 'Sometimes when I get home, phone my friends and ask them if they fancy coming out for the evening I feel a bit out of place when they say they can't because they are going out with their girlfriends or they say they will but can they bring their girlfriend too. That's when it strikes you what a different kind of life you lead. But maybe tomorrow we might meet the girl of our dreams. Maybe tomorrow we might fall madly in love.'

There are some advantages: 'I enjoy the idea of all these different girls liking me. It's a great buzz,' admits Mark. 'I love the attention of the fans. But don't get us wrong, we don't go about looking to make love to anything that moves. It's not like that at all.'

Jason, too, says his attitude to girls has changed since he joined the band. 'I'm sure one day I'll have a nice family and settle down. But at the moment I am used to living like this. Though I've had girlfriends in the past they've not really been steady.'

The one member of the band whose romantic life hasn't changed is the youngest, Robbie Williams. 'I have never had a steady girlfriend,' he confesses. 'The longest I have ever been out with anybody is three weeks. Long-term relationships are not me.

'All our class were out with different people all

the time. You'd be going out with this person this week and that person the next week, and that happened all through school. When I left school I joined the band, and there was no time for a steady relationship.

'Do I miss having a relationship? I don't know. Besides, you can't really miss something you've never had.'

FAN-TASTIC

The faithful followers

Take That's army of followers are the largest and most loyal of all British fans – at the time of writing the band's fan club totalled a staggering 70,000 members.

And the adulation that they lavish on the band can get scary at times. In August 1992, three months before the band set off on their series of British concerts, they began a tour of HMV record shops. The tour had to be scrapped after the band visited a store in Manchester and were besieged by 5,000 fans. In the end the band had to be smuggled out!

The incident in Manchester was just an example of the hysteria that Take That has caused throughout Britain, and which is now spreading all over the world. Sometimes the consequences can be distressing for the band and the fans. 'We had to stop doing small clubs and personal appearances in leisure centres because it really did get too dangerous,' says Gary. 'We had a lot of trouble with the police when we were doing our signings so we decided to give up on them for a while. But we were upset when the police decided we shouldn't do any appearances because a lot of fans think it was our decision. At that time we got a lot of mail from fans asking why we cancelled, saying "without us you would be nothing". What they didn't understand was it wasn't us who called those appearances off.

'Some fans thought that we'd had enough and we didn't want to do those places, but nothing could have been further from the truth. One of the most lasting impressions I have is the story of a girl who had spent hundreds of pounds on clothes and presents and stood outside a venue for four hours, only to find that it had been called off. Our fans are wonderfully loyal and we would never do anything to upset them.'

There have been some scary moments for the band. Mark remembers one time in Bristol: 'We were leaving the leisure centre and it was really a case of us running for our lives to the van which was parked nearby. The fans were going wild, chasing madly after us. But when we got to the van, we thought we'd had it – the van was locked and there was nobody in it.

'We were badly scratched before we were saved

by our crew who bundled us into the van.'

'Another time we were doing a personal appearance in a shopping centre,' recalls Robbie, 'where the crowd, who were really close to us, got carried away. Normally I put my hand out to them and then withdraw it really quickly, but this time it didn't work. When I went to try to whisk my hand away they grabbed hold of it and they pulled me forward. I fell right into the crowd. I thought I was going to get smothered, but luckily our helpers came to the rescue.'

Another time, the band were being pursued by a hoard of fans in their home town and tried to escape by dashing into a local shopping centre – only to be thrown out by the security guards!

The band are also deluged by thousands of fan letters from girls, writing about everything under the sun. Some letters just ask for autographs, others for sex, while still others say how miserable their lives are and how they want to end it all.

'We get all sorts of fan mail,' says Mark. 'It is quite staggering. They tell us about their most private thoughts and feelings. It's quite amazing how much they open up to us. With some of those letters you really feel you know the person that is writing to you because they bare their soul.

'It's difficult, of course, to answer all the letters.

At one point we tried to answer a number of them personally but sometimes we just don't have the time to answer as many as we'd like. But our helpers sift through the letters and give us a number to read, saying if you are going to answer any this week, try your best to answer these ones.'

Take That's pretty-boy looks and athletic dance routines have won them a lot of gay fans. From the early days the band performed in gay clubs and those shows, together with the fact that no member of the band has a steady girlfriend, led to the inevitable, though wrong, rumours that the band might be gay. 'The rumours started because I've always insisted that the boys play in gay clubs,' admits Nigel. 'They are five good-looking lads so the gay clubs always offered a lot more than the straight clubs. My attitude was why not?'

Performing in gay clubs was certainly an eye-opener for Gary who admits that he – like the other guys in the band – was chatted up all the time. 'We've always done gay clubs and people always used to cheer and wolf-whistle when we'd go on stage. Before the band I didn't know anything about gay people, their views or how they lived. But now I feel I've lived a whole lot more.

'Guys would chat us up all the time and they were quite forward. They'd want to know if I was

gay and when I said "I'm not" they used to say "That's cool" and keep on talking.'

The gay rumours posed no problem for any of the band members. Says Mark: 'I like gay rumours because it just creates a bit of mystery about the band. We also get a lot of letters from gay men saying they fancy us but we're not bothered by that.'

'We basically play to people who like our music,' adds Howard, 'and we just happen to have a big gay following. I don't see what's wrong with that.'

When the band decided to support AIDS charities it only strengthened the gay rumours, but they felt it was important to do their bit.

'There are a lot of important charities to support,' says Robbie, 'but AIDS is really worrying. We wanted to do this as kids often listen to us when they don't listen to teachers.'

The band are genuinely concerned for their army of fans. They know that without them they would not have the success they enjoy and they believe that too many pop stars forget that their fans are real people and instead regard them simply as a means of buying themselves the latest luxuries and maintaining their 'superstar' lifestyle.

When I interviewed Gary after their first Newcastle show, he wasn't interested in what the critics thought – he was much more eager to know whether their fans had enjoyed the performance.

He asked me: 'Did you speak to the fans last night? What were their reactions? It seemed to me like we weren't on that long. Were they moaning about how long we were on for?'

Gary and the rest of the band are determined to remain loyal to the fans who supported their pop career before they even had any chart hits.

'I love the adulation from the girls,' said Gary. 'Sometimes I wish we could get closer, sometimes I wish we could just sit and talk to them all night. I just hope that feeling never goes. I know we won't ever think we're too big time to stand and talk to them but people around us might try and pull away.'

Mark, whose boyish looks have made him the band's supreme pin-up and won him the attention of thousands of fans, adds: 'One of the main things that we have tried to ensure about the band is that we are approachable to our fans and to have constant contact with them.'

Since Take That shot to fame the fans have developed curious ways of expressing their feelings towards the band members. Mark explains: 'The fans picked up different ways of reacting to all our songs. When we were singing "Satisfied"

there were Marathons and chocolate bars being thrown on stage. On "Give Good Feeling" we sing a line where we fly, fly, fly and they all made paper planes which they used to throw at us.

'And when we did a gig in York it was clear that all the fans had been planning something together. As soon as we started the last song they all bombarded us with teddy bears and streamers and spray foam. All the road crew came up on the stage and danced with us.'

Take That's fans are so hooked on the band that they will travel hundreds of miles to camp outside their homes dotted around Manchester and Cheshire. But according to Mark, some fans are more desirable than others. 'We do have both possessive fans and ones who we just see occasionally. They are all nice, although I think it's a bit unfair when we're followed everywhere by someone, especially when it's to our homes!

'That's what some of the more possessive ones do. At one point there were so many fans outside my home that I thought I should move out to give the neighbours some peace and quiet. But now I'm away from home so often, they know about it and don't come and wait outside so much. Now my dad is much happier about the state of affairs and has even been talking about selling off a few bricks has even been talking about selling off a few bricks from the family home as fan souvenirs! I hope he's joking.

'One of the things that constantly amazes me about the fans is how they seem to know our every move. They know when we are flying out of the country, know when we are coming back to Britain and even know what hotels we stay in.'

Take That won an army of British fans in 1992 and in 1993 they set off around the world in search of more troops. They didn't have any problems in attracting new recruits.

ONWARDS AND UPWARDS

Success for Take That

For Take That, 1992 ended with a string of triumphs.

In November they showed how they were dominating the British pop scene when their new single 'Could It Be Magic' reached number 3 in the charts and stayed in the Top Five throughout December. They had yet more success in December when their compilation video *Take That And Party* became the best-selling music video of 1992, even though it had only been on sale for just three weeks and was competing against videos that had been on release throughout the whole of the year. Released on 7 December 1992, the video entered the charts at number 1 and stayed there.

The band added to their run of success when they walked away with a staggering seven top prizes at the *Smash Hits* Awards. Among the prizes they picked up were Best Group, Best Single, Best LP and Best Video. The band that had been the previous year's favourites, New Kids on the Block, failed to pick up any awards. The ultimate humiliation came when New Kids' Jordan Knight had to present one of the prizes to the Manchester idols.

After the ceremony, which was screened live from London's Olympia Arena, Mark Owen told me: 'This time last year we were wondering if we'd ever make it. I can't believe this has happened to us. It's wonderful.' Later that night Take That celebrated their success at a star-studded party at L'Equipe Anglais club in London's West End where they were the toast of the night.

It was the perfect end to a triumphant year for Take That, and helped to make up for a lot of the criticism they have taken in the past. The road to fame hasn't always been an easy one for the band and they have had many harsh words written about them. One of their critics who has since changed his mind is Pete Waterman, pop mogul and presenter of *The Hitman and Her*. When Take That were struggling to win a record company deal they approached Waterman but he turned them down.

'Their version of pop music was not my version of pop music,' he says. 'I take my music very seriously and I don't believe that, at that time, they did. I found them too manufactured. But that was

three years ago and they've changed a lot since then. They have had three years of working non-stop and that has really shaped them up. If they didn't have a deal and they came to me now, I would sign them up straight away.'

Gary admits he was disappointed when Waterman turned them down: 'I've always loved the Stock, Aitken and Waterman stuff. In fact, when I first started writing songs, I used to try to write mine just like theirs. So it was a bit of a blow when he said no.'

When people refused to believe in Take That it simply made the band even more determined to succeed. 'Pop music was very out when we started our career,' says Gary. 'That's why we struggled so much at the beginning. When we told people about our songs and the kind of group we were they reacted as if we were lepers. People accused us of having no talent and said we couldn't sing. I remember the first time we did *Top of the Pops* the camera crew and a lot of other production staff were having bets about whether we could even sing. But that just spurred us on. When I got up on stage at the BBC I just sang my heart out. Yes, it does make you want to try harder.'

The band spent Christmas with their families, and jetted off to Europe in the New Year to do some promotional work. Then, one cold day in January Take That received some heart-warming news. They had been nominated for two prizes – Best British Newcomers and Single of the Year – at Britain's most prestigious awards show, the BRITS, the rock equivalent of Hollywood's Oscars. The BRITS are a yearly event where the superstars of rock battle it out against each other and any act that is nominated can truly say they have arrived.

1992's BRITS were announced at one of London's most popular hangouts, the Hard Rock Café. Take That were in exalted company that day: among the nominees were such stars as Elton John, Eric Clapton, Mick Hucknall and Madonna. The band were so thrilled to be nominated that they even turned up to the restaurant that morning where they mingled with other celebrities and posed happily in front of a huge cardboard cut-out of the BRITS symbol.

At the time Robbie told me: 'I think what particularly thrilled us about being nominated for the best British newcomer award was that it is chosen by people in the music business, a lot of the big chiefs, so we were really pleased that those kinds of people were taking us seriously. For some reason people in the business seem to be more in favour of rock and indie acts, things which

they see as being supposedly more serious and more credible, so getting the nomination was wonderful.'

But only a few weeks later their BRITS triumph had been shattered. Despite being nominated, the fivesome were snubbed by the organizers when they were not invited to perform at the awards ceremony. The band's reaction was understandably angry. 'I couldn't care less about the BRITS. They don't mean anything to me,' said Jason. 'People in the music industry don't seem to care about a young band like us. The awards the public vote for are the ones the bands are more interested in.'

A friend of the band said: 'I can't believe Take That won't be there. They've been one of the biggest bands of the year and the newest. The BRITS have often been criticized for being a redundant dinosaur and this is further proof. I've heard that Madness are one of the acts performing at the show. They were all right ten years ago but they're not exactly "now", are they?'

But Nigel Martin-Smith was not surprised that Take That had been left out in the cold by the organizers. 'I had a bet with the boys that they'll not win the categories they've been nominated for. I told them that they were not credible enough even though they were obviously the best newcomers. They have sold loads of records, a million singles, half a million albums. As far as I was concerned, they were the most successful act of the year. But that is one of the things that really upsets me about the business, there is so much pretentiousness in it.'

But the band did win a prize although it was one of the few awards not chosen by chiefs of the British music industry. They romped home in the Best Single category with their song 'Could It Be Magic', chosen by polling listeners of Radio 1.

Instead of going to the BRITS the band decided to take off for America. The band had conquered Britain and were ready to take on the rest of the world. Already all the signs of world domination were there. The band's records had begun selling wildly all over Europe – Germany, France, Spain and Sweden were already showing signs of full-scale fan worship.

In an interview I did with the band just after they had come back from a promotional tour of the continent they described the scenes of mass hysteria they had witnessed. Mark had even got a 'smashing' black eye from one frenzied fan. 'We came out of a TV studio in Stockholm and were mobbed by two hundred girls,' he told me. 'They just went crazy, they got so carried away, especi-

ally this one girl who whacked me in the eye with her camera. It was a total accident, she was swinging her arms around madly and hit me in the face. It hurt like anything for hours and for the next few days I was walking around with a real shiner.

'But the fans have been really great wherever we have gone. We're learning that fans are the same all over the world although our British fans will always have a special place in our hearts because they are the ones who made us. We couldn't have done it without them. We are thrilled at how well everything is going for us. We just don't know how we are going to have time to fit everything in.

'One thing we've noticed is that abroad a lot of guys have been turning up to see us. That's good. I think at the end of the day they see us over there as just a group and we should be able to have fans of all ages and of both sexes. I think that is happening here too, now.'

The band are learning to deal with spending more time abroad. When I met them after their trip to the continent, Gary had celebrated his birthday in Germany and Mark had his in Sweden. They also shot a video for their single 'Why Can't I Wake Up With You' in France. 'The video was shot about thirty miles outside Paris in an old chateau,' says Gary. 'It was gorgeous. We wanted to get a very moody feel for the video and we hope we succeeded. Actually, the place we were in – though it was nice – was very boring. We sat around for three days really doing nothing, just waiting to do our shoot. There was a moat around the chateau which was all frozen up and we used to play dare devil games and see who could walk the furthest on the lake. We were all egging each other on, but luckily no one fell in.'

'The highlight of the week was finding a dead stoat frozen up in the ice,' adds Robbie. 'We used to go and sing songs to it because that was the only interesting thing to do. It was very desolate. There was only one restaurant and that didn't have a great choice of food. We went there every night and had the same meal. If we hadn't been working there perhaps we could have taken advantage of the beauty and peacefulness of the place but so much of the time was spent just hanging around waiting to be filmed for our various scenes.' The single, 'Why Can't I Wake Up With You', was a smash success, rocketing to number 2 in the charts in the first week of its release.

Over the last few months their gruelling schedule has become even more hectic. 'It's a bit like if it's Monday it must be Spain,' laughs Gary. 'Sometimes we've been to four different countries in four

days. It sounds glamorous when you read about it, but it is actually very hard work. When we went over to Germany for three days recently we started work at nine in the morning and didn't stop till midnight. But it's something we know we have to do. We're thankful that people like us so much. We realize that we could be working as hard in every country as we did in Britain. The other day I got back from somewhere or other, I can't even remember the country, and couldn't wait to jump into my bed. I fell asleep on Sunday at five in the evening and the next thing I knew the phone was ringing and it was ten minutes past four the next afternoon.'

The band are very aware that their newfound success all over the world – Europe, America and Japan – will take them away from their British fans for a while. It is something that worries them a great deal. 'We all worry about leaving England for too long,' says Gary. 'We know that it is important for us to be successful in other countries, every group has to move on, but we will certainly never desert Britain and our wonderful fans here. We have worked so hard to get them, and they have been so loyal that we don't want to do anything to disappoint them. We think about them all the time.'

Mark has similar views: 'There are far too many bands who have a few hits in Britain and then decide they've got what it takes to conquer the world and consequently leave all their old fans behind. We will never do that.'

▲ An early picture of the talented fivesome, fresh-faced and hopeful

▼ Spot the extrovert!

▲ The band model their original leather look ▼

▲ 'How does this go on?' asks a puzzled Jason. 'I haven't a clue,' says Howard

▲ Mark begs for mercy as the band shoot the video for 'Do What U Like', while Howard and Jason bend over backwards to please ▼

▲ Take That in a party mood and getting out and about ▼

▲ A steamy shot, their bodies glistening with sweat and – red jelly?

▼ Robbie seems to have bitten off more than he can chew

▸ Could Gary be on the phone to his hairdresser?

◂ A pre-beard Jason smiles sweetly for the camera

▲ Mark – and *that* grin

▲ Howard, break-dancer extraordinaire, gives us his enigmatic look

NUMBER ONE!

Take That hit the top of the charts

A few months after the disappointment of the BRITS came pure joy for Take That. They got what they had been dreaming, wishing, hoping and praying for ever since they started – a number one single. The single was 'Pray' and it showed everyone in Britain what the fans already knew – that Take That were our top band. But before 'Pray' hit the number one spot, there was more globetrotting to be done.

In May of 1993, Take That made their second assault on America, the one country where success still eluded them. The previous few months had seen them conquer and captivate the rest of Europe as well as Australia and the Far East. As the five-some landed in New York they were full of memories of the countries that had become part of the ever-expanding Take That world. They had been overwhelmed by the devotion of their new fans. Robbie Williams recalled how the Japanese fans would even book expensive rooms in some of

Japan's poshest hotels, where a mere soft drink can cost £5, to be close to their idols.

'Even when we got the famous bullet train from Tokyo we couldn't shake them off,' he recalled. 'There must have been around 300 fans travelling on that train after they found out we were getting it, just to get a glimpse of us. It was amazing, it must have cost them £200 each.'

Of course, being in foreign countries created a language barrier between the boys and their fans, as Mark Owen recalled. He described how Jason Orange had tried his hand at chatting up some of Spain's beautiful senoritas but failed spectacularly. 'Jason had been swotting up on his Spanish with a phrase book but got himself in a terrible muddle. He was surrounded by a lot of girls in the hotel and decided to say "good morning" to them. He got his words mixed up and instead bid them *mañana* which isn't "good morning" but "tomorrow". So the girls left baffled and very confused!'

Take That's New York trip was very different to their first visit to the city, which had had them hungering for more than just fame. On the very first day their American record company had given them some money and the boys assumed that it was their daily allowance. 'We went out and blew

the whole lot on clothes and souvenirs,' Robbie recalled. 'We didn't realise it was meant to buy us our meals and food for the whole two weeks we were there. Towards the end of that trip we were really starving.'

During their times in New York, the lads' feet hardly touched the ground. They loved the exciting and frenzied atmosphere of the city, but admitted finding it scary, too.

'Whenever you put on the telly there is all this news about murders and shootings and it does affect you,' said Robbie. 'We're not the bravest of guys – in fact we're right softies – so when we found ourselves in Central Park, which can be a pretty violent place, as darkness set in, we really panicked. We got very frightened that we were going to get mugged and beaten up and legged it out of there as fast as we could. Linford Christie would have had nothing on us that day!'

In June 1993, Take That fans saw Gary Barlow advertising the delights of chewing gum. But the ads, which appeared in a string of teenage magazines, showed a very young Gary indeed, not the hunky heart-throb he is today. The picture showed a bleached blond Gary, silver and blue streaks in his hair, with a strip of Stimorol gum clenched between his pearly white teeth. It was made before Gary had become a pop star and had been consigned to the archives until somebody at the company remembered the hidden treasure that lay in their vaults – a treasure all the more valuable because though Take That do allow their tours to be sponsored, none of the members have ever appeared in adverts while they were in the group.

It seems Stimorol had recognised star qualities in the young singer. 'Gary was chosen for the ad because he had the right image and pop stars looks, even though he wasn't one at the time,' said a spokesman for the company. A shamefaced Gary admitted, 'I did the ad for a bit of a laugh, although I really don't like chewing gum.'

Gary wasn't the only member of the band to find his past hitting the headlines. Jason Orange's father, Tony, revealed that the star was lucky to be alive, having missed death by inches as a baby. Jason's mum had moved his cot from the bay window of their Manchester home just seconds before a lintel collapsed. The spot were Jason had been sleeping just a few moments earlier was showered by tons of rubble.

'It was a lucky escape,' said Tony. Thousands of young girls agreed.

*

On July 11, Take That stormed straight to the number one with their single 'Pray'. The song, which was to become one of the band's classics, was accompanied by a moody video, shot in the paradise holiday resort of Acapulco in Mexico.

Just days after 'Pray' hit the number one spot, Take That kicked off a brand new sell-out tour in their home town of Manchester. They were set to rake in a staggering £1.2 million from just six shows, thanks to a combination of ticket sales and lucrative merchandising. But the band were being incredibly generous with the money they were making. All the profits from one of the shows at Manchester's G-Mex were going to Manchester's Children's Hospital as part of the Bryan Robson scanner appeal.

The tour saw Take That playing to the biggest audiences ever, with 8,000 screaming fans flocking to each show at the G-Mex Centre. I was there on the first night and I could not help but be amazed by the sheer size and spectacle of it all. Here was a band who just a year and a half ago were playing to handfuls of people in small clubs. Their rise to stardom had been truly meteoric.

The show opened with two bright blue search-lights scanning and swaying over the audience. Suddenly the group appeared and launched into

'Take That And Party'. What followed was a scintillating cocktail of the three 'S's – Sex, Style and Smash Hits. Sex effervesced throughout their show in their bedroom banter and sensual moves. Style spilled over with their spectacular stage effects, while the smash songs were there in sheer abundance.

The concert ended on an extremely cheeky note. After an encore of 'It Only Takes A Minute' the band pulled down their trousers to reveal Take That written in big letters on the backs of the underpants.

After the opening night, the band invited me to party with them at a local Manchester hotspot, Cruz 101. It was a wild night and the band were on top of the world. All their families were there, in fact, it felt like one big happy family. The only sign of anxiety was from the group's perennial worrier, Mark, who was concerned that his mum might think his performance was too raunchy. But Mrs Owen gave it the thumbs up.

As always, Take That put their fans first. They were so concerned about the fans' safety that they laid on an extra 20 security guards at every show. The added protection was the brainchild of Take That's quick-thinking manager, Nigel Martin-Smith. He realised that the thousands of young

girls that each one of the band's shows attracted could be a magnet for all kinds of perverts. During a plush backstage party at London's Wembley Arena to celebrate the tour, Martin-Smith told me, 'Although many of the girls are brought to and from the show by their parents, we didn't want to take any chances. We stepped up our security and had them patrolling each venue, keeping an eye out for anything out of the ordinary. The guards would ask groups of girls if any of them had been approached by strange men outside and also tell them not to talk to any strange men.

'A lot of fans hang around all day, hours before the band go on stage as well as after they have come off stage, to try to get a glimpse of the group – so we thought it was essential to have our guards keeping an eye on them at all times. The security worked well. As far as I know there was only one incident which happened in Manchester when a man was arrested after telling a very young girl he could take her to the hotel where the band were staying.'

Take That's stageshows were getting sexier and sexier. In August 1993 they got themselves into a spot of hot water when they staged a saucy strip-tease at a charity concert in aid of the children's charity Childline. The strip featured the band dropping their trousers to reveal the word Childline written in big black letters across the back of their undies. Each member of the band had huge letters spelling out the name of the charity on his backside and when they turned their backs to the audience, the word Childline struck all the girls in the audience right between the eyes.

The papers reported that chiefs of the agency, which was started by TV presenter Esther Rantzen, were upset by the band's antics, even though the group raised £60,000 for them. Defending the strip, Gary Barlow said, 'We wanted to give Childline the maximum publicity we could. We felt this was a great and fun way in which to do that. We knew that would get our point across and keep the charity in every fan's mind.' Mark Owen added, 'Childline is a wonderful charity and we are only too happy to help them. It's the kids who put us here today and it's important to give something back to them.'

In the same month, That Take averted what could have been an horrific tragedy at a concert in Chelmsford, Essex. The show, playing to 25,000 people, turned to terror when screaming fans were crushed by the thousands surging forward to be closer to their idols. Though 32 girls were taken to hospital and a further 100 needed First Aid,

a worse tragedy was prevented when Take That stopped their performance and urged fans to calm down and move back. Gary Barlow pleaded with the crowd, 'People are getting hurt. We can't go on unless you all move back.'

Afterwards police paid tribute to the band for calming the crowd and preventing many more injuries. A source said, 'The responsible behaviour of the band prevented what could have been a very serious incident.' Describing what it had been like in the crush, fan Jane Mason said, 'It was terrifying when everyone pushed forward. I thought someone was going to die.'

A few weeks earlier there had been a similar incident at a show at Crystal Palace as part of National Music Day. On that occasion the baking heat, with temperatures rising to the mid–70s, and the crush among the crowd of 30,000, resulted in 600 people needing medical treatment, mainly for heat exhaustion, with 30 being taken to hospital.

In October 1993, I was able to reveal the news that all Take That fans had been waiting for – their two-year ban on having any steady girlfriends was over. But it seemed that Take That were in no hurry to make up for lost time and settle down with Miss Right. They told me that they were going to extend the ban on girlfriends themselves, voluntarily, because they still had a lot to achieve in their careers and wanted to put that first.

'Originally the no-girlfriends ban was our manager's idea,' explained Gary. 'He thought that having regular girlfriends would be a distraction to our career. He thought that we would be torn between our love for them and our love for our music and that inevitably the music would take second place to our girls. But he didn't want us to live like monks and be celibate so he told us that he didn't mind us making love as long as nothing developed into a relationship. It was a tough rule but the group was very important to us and we could see his point and his reasoning. More than anything we wanted the group to succeed so we went along with his idea. And he was right. For almost the last two years we have been able to concentrate solely on our career and dedicate ourselves to it and our career has been incredible so far.

'Now the ban is up but there are still new areas we want to conquer, lots of things we want to achieve and that will involve a lot of hard work, so we are going to give girlfriends a miss for a while longer. We are going to extend the ban ourselves. It is going to be very difficult because there are so

many beautiful women around and you can get very lonely, but we know it makes sense.'

Every member of Take That told me they wanted to settle down with the right girl and have children. 'Each and every one of us is getting broody,' Jason admitted. 'We would all like to have kids. That's something we've all been thinking about a lot. We spend a lot of time talking about what it would be like to be dads and the broodiness increases because a lot of our friends who we grew up with have babies now and you can't help but put yourself in their position. But for the time being, fatherhood is another thing we will have to give a miss to.'

During my interview with the band, Mark's thoughts also turned to romance and he told me he believed Take That fans were getting more and more beautiful. 'I don't know what it is, or why, but the Take That fans have been getting more and more gorgeous. It could be because they are getting older, they are growing up as we are growing up. The girls that were once fledglings are now glamorous women. It's very exciting. When we are doing shows and we look out on the sea of faces and bodies in our audiences you can't help but notice how some of them are real crackers. We seem to have fans of all ages now. When we go travelling we know that some of the airline hostesses and stewardesses we meet must be real fans because they shake and tremble when they meet us. If people think our fans are just pubescent girls, they couldn't be more wrong.'

On 8 November Take That embarked on another British tour, this time kicking off in the seaside resort of Bournemouth. Again the tour was an instant sell-out and it was calculated that the group would rake in the majestic sum of £2 million from the 21 dates. The number of fans the band were now playing to was further proof of their growing success.

Once again the fans found it hard to control themselves when the band launched into their exciting new stage show. Around 200 fans fainted in the heat and excitement of that first show, which dazzled the capacity crowd of 4,000. One fan, Hayley Costello, 11, said after the show ended, 'One minute I was screaming and shouting, the next I just keeled over. When I came around I was in the First Aid area lying alongside dozens of other girls.'

One of the many high-spots of the show was Jason Orange's transformation into a beautiful young woman. He looked so convincing that many

of the fans thought it was a real girl who was a new ingredient in the band's act. Jason fooled everyone, leaving them open-mouthed when he suddenly appeared on stage looking like a cross between rock's raunchiest female star Madonna and Hollywood legend Marilyn Monroe. Dressed in a fetching blue and white polka-dot dress and a shoulder length peroxide blonde wig adorned with a pretty matching bow, the chisel-cheeked star did a smoochy dance on stage with Howard Donald. It was Take That's own version of the Olivia Newton-John and John Travolta dance routine from the movie *Grease* and the fans adored it.

Afterwards Jason came clean about his cross-dressing antics. 'It was my own idea. I thought it would be great fun and it was. I have never dressed up in women's clothes before, but I wanted to do something zany, and this is definitely the zaniest thing I have ever done. I think I looked like a bit of all right, though there was one slight problem – having to remember to do the woman's steps in the dance routine.'

The stunning stage show included some of the band's biggest hits, among them 'Pray', 'It Only Takes A Minute', 'Why Can't I Wake Up With You' and their recent number one smash hit 'Relight My Fire'. The band were as determined as ever to give the audience real value for money and spared no expense to give a colourful, fast-paced extravaganza. Their performance featured them in seven costume changes which included hooded monks' habits, trench coats and trilbys as well as the casual uniform of white T-shirts and jeans. Jason Orange not only wore the best dress in the whole of the show, but also the sexiest gear of the tour – a see-through yellow top and figure-hugging black leather shorts.

As the band got raunchier in their stage show, so did their devoted fans. At the Bournemouth concert hundreds of fans paraded sexily suggestive placards to catch the band's attention. One pleaded, 'We want your sex. Make it with us tonight.'

But Take That were very aware of the serious side to all this. One of the things the band wanted to do on the tour was a benefit show for an AIDS charity. All the boys believe that AIDS is something that teenagers need to be very aware of. Gary told me, 'It's a very important cause and something we have always been concerned about. We have known a few people who have died from AIDS and I'm sure we'll know a good few more before the decade finishes. We realise we have a very young following and as pop stars we are aware

that we have a responsibility to them. We believe it's vitally important that they learn about AIDS at the same time as they learn about sex. It's not very nice that that has to be part of their education, but that's the climate that today's kids live in. It's very sad but AIDS is something that you can't brush under the carpet.'

Not long afterwards, however, Take That found their position as role models for the young getting them into trouble. A few days after the British tour began, the band made an amazing revelation which many saw as part of the group's desire to create a more mature image for themselves. Three of the group's members, Howard Donald, Jason Orange and Robbie Williams, admitted they had experimented with drugs – though they were quick to point out that their dabblings were only tiny, isolated incidents. The revelations came when the band was interviewed by one of Britain's trendiest magazines, *The Face*. 'I'm not going to lie and say I've not taken drugs,' said Robbie, while Jason confessed, 'I have experimented. But I realised I didn't need it and I'm no longer curious about the effects.' Howard revealed, 'I used to go raving and I tried half an acid [LSD] but it did nothing. That's all I've taken.'

Gary Barlow and Mark Owen lived up to the

band's squeaky clean image, however, saying they had never tried drugs. Gary even admitted that he had never smoked because he was frightened it might harm his voice.

The group's drug confession was attacked by a a number of people in the medical field. Leading drug expert Professor Colin Pritchard called them 'irresponsible' for their stance over experimentation with drugs. He also said that many young people would look up to their idols for a lead on such matters. But a source close to the band hit back, saying, 'The band just wanted to be honest and not lie about a subject like that. But it was a one-off experience and in no way do they condone drug taking. They know that drugs are dangerous.'

1993 ended on a high note for the Take That. At the beginning of December the band showed how much they dominated the British pop scene by scooping an incredible eight prizes at a glittering awards ceremony run by top teenage magazine *Smash Hits*, beating their previous year's record of seven awards. Among the prizes the group won were Best Group in the World and Best British Group. The band's LP 'Everything Changes' won the best album award and the single 'Pray' won the best video award. The boys were ecstatic. 'This

is absolutely fantastic,' said Gary after the record-breaking bonanza. 'We feel as if we are on top of the world.'

In mid December Take That went into the pop record books when their new single 'Babe', featuring Mark on vocals, went straight into the number one spot in the charts. It meant that Take That became the first act in British pop history to score three instant chart-toppers with successive singles. 'Babe', followed in the footsteps of 'Pray' and 'Relight My Fire', both of which debuted at number one. It knocked off the novelty song 'Mr Blobby', sung by the pink and yellow blob who became cult TV viewing on Noel Edmond's House Party. But Blobby got his own back on the group when his record went back to the coveted number one spot at Christmas, no doubt thanks to the cloth-eared grans and granpas and children under five who went out to buy this piece of nonsense.

But despite 'Babe' slipping to the number two position, when the round-up of 1993's best selling pop singles, albums and videos of the year came out, Take That had plenty to crow about. They found themselves with two of the top ten best-selling singles of the year, 'Babe' and 'Pray', and the tenth best-selling album of the year, 'Everything Changes'. Best of all, their two videos, *Take*

That and Party and *The Party – Live At Wembley* were the number one and number two best-selling videos of the year. There was no doubt, Take That had arrived.

BY ROYAL APPOINTMENT

Success brings the boys face to face with royalty

In 1994 Take That mania showed no signs of stopping, forcing those sceptics who believed teenage bands only had a lifespan of a couple of years to eat their words. Pop history had shown that acts who appealed to the notoriously fickle teen market were almost always dismissed by their fans all too soon – as the examples of former big idols Bros and Rick Astley showed. Yet Take That had confounded history, refusing to be slaves to it. By the beginning of 1994, the band had been having top ten hits for nearly two years, and were getting more and more successful by the week.

As the boys' fame grew and grew, they became aware of the difficulties such success inevitably brought to those close to them. In February Robbie's mum, Theresa, pinned a note to the front door of her home in Stoke-on-Trent, where her pop idol son still lived when he wasn't working. The note, written in blue felt tip, read, 'Dear fans, thanks for calling. I am sorry, but Rob isn't home now. In fact he has had to spend some time away because he is not getting any privacy. It would be very considerate of you if you would not knock and disturb us. With love and thanks, Mrs Williams.'

Robbie's sister Julie revealed, 'It's our mum who suffers the most because she is here all the time, while Robbie and I aren't. Fans never stop knocking on the door and mum never gets any peace.'

In the same month, the band staged one of their biggest coups when they performed live at the prestigious BRITS, the glittering awards ceremony which had snubbed them a year earlier. The band left the star-studded audience – which included Elton John, Bono, Jon Bon Jovi, Seal, Bjork, former Labour leader Neil Kinnock and footballers Ian Wright, Paul Merson and Paul Ince - amazed with their homage to the best band Britain has ever produced, the Beatles. Dressed in 60s Beatles clothes – high-buttoned, electric-blue mohair suits and white buttoned- down shirts – their hair brushed forward in mop-top style, they pumped out a Beatles medley which included such classic Fab Four tunes as 'I Wanna Hold Your Hand' and 'She Loves You'.

It was a performance that could have gone disastrously wrong – a band imitating the legends of

British pop in front of an audience full of middle-aged people who revered the Beatles. But the weeks of secret rehearsals paid off and Take That went down a storm. They won themselves a whole new audience that night – the BRITS were watched on TV by around ten million people – as well as earning the admiration and respect music industry bigwigs. The Fab Five's interpretation of the Fab Four also introduced a whole generation of young fans to the music of the Beatles.

Afterwards the band explained, 'We weren't trying to be cheeky. We all really love the Beatles and wanted to pay our own humble tribute to them.' Gary Barlow added, 'People thought we were comparing ourselves to the Beatles, but we weren't. We do think we have some things in common, though. The Beatles were a group that believed in having fun and a laugh and that's what we've always tried to do.'

The bigger Take That grew, the more rumours about its members flew. In the early part of 1994 a rumour began that left many Take That fans devastated and heartbroken. It was said that the band's most musically talented member, Gary Barlow, was planning a solo career away from the band. It was speculation that had been going around the music industry for a number of months. The reasoning behind it was that a teen group only has a limited lifespan after which they are dead and buried – if Gary Barlow, who had proved himself one of the 90s' biggest songwriting talents, wanted to keep going, he would have to create a career for himself outside the band. But Gary was quick to jump on the rumour and blast it as untrue. 'That's rubbish,' he said. 'I'm not leaving. People always try to put the boot into anything that is successful. For ages a lot of folk were saying this band wouldn't last. We have proved them wrong, so now they are saying that I'm leaving. Well, I'm not. How long this band will stay together is down to just one thing and it's a very simple thing. As long as the fans want us, that's how long we'll be here.'

Many bands start to take it easy when they get their first sniff of success. They reckon that they have worked hard to claw their way out of the jungle where unknown bands battle to get that foothold into the charts and now they can relax, and take it easy, enjoying the trappings of success. And when acts get the kind of phenomenal success that Take That have won, the temptations to rest on your laurels and take some time out to spend your hard-earned cash is even greater. But that life did not appeal to Take That. In fact the more

success they had, the harder they worked.

1994 was a particularly gruelling year for the band. In March they set off on a demanding European tour, playing to over 100,000 fans in countries including Germany, Holland and Sweden. 'Working abroad is very hard and can be really gruelling,' said Gary, 'especially when you have a schedule that is as hectic and tight as our one. The work is non-stop, but once you get yourself on stage and you hear the cheers of the crowd it makes it all worth it. Before our European tour we played a one-off in Germany and the crowd just went mad. But we are very nervous about this tour, we wouldn't be human if we weren't. This is bigger than anything we have ever done in Europe.'

Every member of the band has their own way of relaxing in the little free time they do have when touring. Gary indulges in his passion for antiques. 'I love going to new places because that's so interesting, but what makes it even more interesting is heading for the local shops to buy antiques and find the best bargains,' he explained. 'I love haggling for bargains. I have bought a lot of different things on these European jaunts including furniture, silver frames and clocks. I love bringing it all back home with me and deciding just where in my home everything is going to go.'

But free time was very rare indeed. In May, rumours raced round the pop world that all the hard work and the pressure that the band were under had resulted in Mark being rushed to hospital. Fans told me, 'We have heard that Mark is very depressed and that the tremendous pressure that the band are under has got to him. The band hardly ever seem to have any time off. All they do is work, work, work constantly. We heard rumours that he had gone to hospital because he feels so down.' But the rumours proved to be unfounded. A spokesman for the band said, 'Mark is in very good health. There is nothing wrong with him. He is not depressed at all. He is currently enjoying himself with the rest of the band in the Far East.'

Mark had certainly been on good form when I spoke to him just before the band set off on tour. The cheeky singer had revealed to me some very bare facts – that the band never slept in pyjamas but liked to hit the hay as naked as nature intended. 'Despite that there have been only a few embarrassing moments,' he added. 'I remember once how some fans caught us naked backstage when they burst in while we were doing a quick costume change. They thought the show had finished and rushed in to congratulate us, only to

see us in all our glory. There were plenty of red faces that day!'

On Monday 28 March the band released the title track of their album 'Everything Changes'. It soared straight to the top of the charts, their fourth successive single to go straight to number one. Not long later, Gary was rewarded with two of the prestigious Ivor Novello awards for his songwriting skills. I was there to see Gary win his trophies and the joy on his face was a delight.

Not everything was going so smoothly, however. Take That's dream of conquering America received a setback when the band and their American record company parted company. The band were unhappy with the backing that the US label had given their only American release, 'It Only Takes A Minute', and decided to hunt around for another record deal.

But nothing could stop Take That's momentum. After the European tour, it was time for Australia, a territory that the boys really loved. Said Gary, 'Australia is a very significant market and it is always somewhere we have wanted to go, so we thought it was about time that we came down here. We had a great time even though we were a bit knackered when we arrived because of our gruelling tour of Europe. Added to that was a 22-hour flight, so I don't know how some of us made it off the plane.'

The trip to Australia proved well worth the effort. It ended with the band performing in front of 3,000 lovesick fans, showing how firmly Take That mania had taken root Down Under.

In August 1994 the band were embarking on their biggest ever British tour – 36 dates, playing to almost 400,000 fans. Just before they began this sell-out British tour at Glasgow's SEEC Centre, I was among the selected handful of people invited to attend a special dress rehearsal for the new stage show. The top secret rehearsal took place in London's Docklands Arena. It was not only a new stage show but a whole new look for the band – their biggest change of image for a long time. With his long, straggly hair dreadlocked, Howard Donald looked like a 60s hippie straight out of Woodstock, while Robbie Williams's cropped black hair gave him the look of an army recruit. Fresh-faced Mark Owen also had a savagely short hair-cut and Jason Orange had grown his hair long, though not quite as crazily as Howard. Gary hadn't done much to change his hair, but he had certainly changed the rest of himself. He had shed the pounds that were making him Take That's

chubbiest member and looked in the best shape he'd been for ages.

Robbie Williams explained the reasoning behind the new image. 'We have all swopped hairstyles,' he said. 'It's – important that way we never get bored with the way we look.'

Talking about the band's upcoming tour, which was to kick off in Scotland the next day, Robbie admitted to some first night nerves. 'This is the biggest tour we've done and to tell you the truth I'm a little nervous, as I know we all are. There are so many special effects on this one and that is a worry because there is a lot more that could go wrong. And it's an expensive outing for us, too. The stage alone costs as much as a big house.'

The band need not have worried: the rehearsal they put on was superb and promised a magical tour. Dressed like Russian foot soldiers, complete with black greatcoats, high Cossack boots and silver helmets, the band kicked off their one and a half hour show with 'Satisfied'. From then on there was no stopping them as they stormed through a parade of smash songs and costume changes. Old favourites were mixed with brand new songs, including the brilliant 'Sure' which was to become their fifth record to go into the chart at number one when it was released in October.

Among the highlights of the show was a Take That tot section, where five young boys who looked uncannily like Take That must have looked in their schooldays – took to the stage. The band and their young lookalikes wore identical outfits of track suits and bomber jackets and went through identical dance routines as they sang one of Take That's earliest hits, 'Do What U Like'. As usual the dancing was a spectacular display of complicated acrobatic routines.

The fast-paced action was perfectly balanced with slower more moody moments. At one point, two pianos rose from the ground for Gary and Howard to duet on, with two of their smoochiest ballads, 'Why Can't I Wake Up With You' and 'A Million Love Songs'.

On a circular platform suspended high up in the air, illuminated by hundreds of lights, the band performed their now famous tribute to the Beatles. Dressed in bright blue 60s style suits they went through a nostalgic medley of the Fab Fours' hits including 'She Loves You', 'I Feel Fine', 'Get Back' and 'Hey Jude'.

Sadly, on the opening night of the tour the band's plans to perform on the circular platform attached to a 140ft walkway suspended from the

ceiling had to be scrapped after Glasgow health and safety officials declared that the most technically adventurous and dazzling part of the group's show was too dangerous and could result in accidents among the huge crowd. Speaking for the band, Mark Owen said, 'We are very disappointed about this. Especially as it is happening on the opening nights of our tour. This is something we have spent a lot of time and money on and we wanted fans from all over the country to see it. But there is nothing we can do. We have to abide by the decision.'

After the Beatles medley things got steamier. For 'Pray' they looked like raunchy monks dressed up in long white dresses which revealed their glistening torsos. Then they changed into string tops, skimpy hot pants and boots for their wild party song 'Give Good Feeling'.

But the steamiest number of all was saved for last, when Howard Donald and the band's guest star Lulu showed off their pert bums. Lulu threw caution to the wind and appeared wearing a see-through red lace dress with a black cutaway corset underneath. Howard revealed more of his honed muscular physique than ever before in a pair of cutaway scarlet leather cowboy chaps and a daring studded leather g-string, allowing everyone to see his bare backside as he bumped and ground suggestively to the number one hit 'Relight My Fire'. Dressed like sexy devils with skimpy outfits and horns on their heads the band sang and danced with Lulu till they were all drenched in so much sweat that they looked as if they had spent an afternoon in hell.

This raunchy finale was to cause a sensation among the fans – and their parents. Some complained that it was just too sexy for the young audience. The band did not agree. 'Everybody seems to be making such a huge deal out of it, but what they're forgetting is that it's just a spot of fun,' said Jason Orange. 'There is no pornography in it. Howard has a very sophisticated bum. I suppose you can't please all the people all the time. People who come to our shows do enjoy them. We're not corrupting anybody.'

Gary defended the new act resolutely, saying, 'People may think we're doing this to shock, but we're not. We're doing it because we want to be different. We don't think our new look is too raunchy for our young fans because it is all done in fun. Everything is tongue in cheek. When Howard shows his bum, it is just a bit of a laugh. We would never do anything to upset our fans.'

The band didn't even think of changing their sexy

show – until, that is, they found themselves playing to royalty. As November gave way to December, the band played to both Prince Charles and Princess Diana in the space of three days. The boys met Prince Charles after recording a Royal Variety Performance and then, on 1 December, they played for Princess Di at an AIDS charity concert at Wembley Arena. Diana, who was escorted to the show by pop star George Michael, smiled and clapped wildly as the band dedicated 'A Million Love Songs' to her, as well as a medley of her favourite Beatles songs.

Originally the band weren't going to include Howard's bum routine for fear of offending the Princess, but Diana had told the shows organisers, 'Don't worry, I like bottoms'. And so it was that Howard gyrated in front of Diana in those infamous leather chaps and g-string.

'We decided to go for it because the Princess seemed game for a laugh,' said Mark. 'I hope she really liked the show because we had the time of our life. We would have loved it if she had got up on stage and danced with us.' Mark admitted that he thought the Princess was gorgeous and that they were all in love with her. Mark was so smitten that he even asked her out on a date!

The day before the concert, Princess Diana had invited the boys to tea at Kensington Palace to

thank them for agreeing to appear and raise money for the AIDS show. Diana knew all about the band – she listened to 'Everything Changes' and had the group's performance on video – and they were soon getting along famously. 'It was wonderful meeting her,' raved Gary afterwards, while Jason declared that he would love to marry her.

As they were drinking tea, Mark flashed his wide-open grin at Diana and boldly asked her, 'Are you free on Sunday, and if so do you fancy going out?' The others looked on in amazement as Diana, who is three inches taller than the cheeky singer, replied, 'Thanks for asking me, but I'm busy that day. I'm sorry.'

Royal put downs aside, 1994 had proved another great year for the irrepressible Take That. They won seven *Smash Hits* awards, including the Greatest Band in the World prize for the third year in a row, as well as the Best Single and the Best Pop Video awards for their smoochy song 'Sure'. Even the fans were making records, the screams that accompanied the group's performance at the *Smash Hits* awards party were measured by the *Guinness Book of Records* as an ear-piercing 115.3 decibels, 15 more decibels than the noise generated by a pneumatic drill!

Few at the awards ceremony could possibly

have guessed that a few months earlier, the band had almost split. The group was devastated when 'Sure', their fifth number one, was knocked off the top of the charts after only two weeks. Take That feared that this could be the beginning of the end for them. They knew they had enjoyed a great run of success and had always resolved to go out on a high, after a number one single, and not when people had stopped buying or listening to their records. The band, who had been left exhausted by their gruelling British tour talked about their future and agreed that they were ready to end Take That.

They were prevented from breaking the hearts of millions of fans all over the world by the man who had guided their career so spectacularly, their manager Nigel Martin-Smith. He convinced Gary to write some new songs, guessing that once Gary started writing, his enthusiasm for the band and all it had achieved, would return.

He was right. That period of writing produced the song that was a milestone in the band's career, a real sea-change. It was 'Back for Good', which was acclaimed by the critics and public alike as one of the best songs of the decade.

The song gave Take That their enthusiasm back, and lead them on to vistas new.

GROWING UP

Take That and their fans grow older, wiser – and sexier!

In February 1995, Take That were back at the BRITS, showcasing their unreleased single 'Back For Good' to a tremendous reception from some of the world's top celebrities and industry bigwigs. It was a milestone record for the band, winning over a whole new older audience and finally silencing those carping critics who said the band were just teen puppets.

'Back For Good' notched up a staggering 500,000 advance orders before it was even released – bigger advance orders than the Band Aid charity record 'Do They Know It's Christmas?' (which had advance orders of 300,000 and went on to sell 3.5 million copies) and shot straight into the number one spot in the charts, confirming Take That's position as the most successful teenage pop band in history. Even such pop idols as Wham could only manage four number one hits in Britain.

Yet the most amazing thing about this beautiful spine-tingling song was that it took Gary only 15 minutes to write. He admitted in Munich in March 1995, after one of the band's European dates, 'I know people think it's quick, but 15 minutes is a long time for me. That included a coffee break. But I do believe that the best songs do come instantly – you don't have to labour over them. I've heard the news about the advance orders and that's just fantastic. Someone has just told me that if you add together all the sales of every single from number two to number 20 at the moment and then double that, it still won't come anywhere near the sales of 'Back For Good'. I'm really amazed and I can't say I'm not happy when I hear things like that.

'Of course I know that much of our success is down to our fantastic fans. Someone recently joked that we could put out a record of ourselves burping and it would probably be a hit and while there's some truth in that I don't want to exploit that. None of us are in this band for easy hits. We don't want to go down that road. We want to make something of quality. I think that one of the things that keeps us going is that we just want to get better and better. I love writing songs. If I could come up with a different way to say "I love you", I'd have a song that would that would sell billions. I feel it's the simple sentiments that work the best.'

'Back for Good' showed a new sophistication

and maturity in Take That, and this was reflected in their changing image. During their European tour they were being dressed by top fashion designers Dolce and Gabbana. The sophisticated new look was evidence that Take That were trying to find a still wider audience for themselves and their music.

'We're growing up and as we get older, Gary's songs mature and that means different people start to like what we're doing,' said Mark Owen. 'We're not saying we want to leave our teenage fans behind. They mean everything to us but like any other band, we want to widen our audience as much as we can. We want everyone to listen to and like our music.'

It wasn't just that Take That's new fans were older, the fans that had been with them from the beginning, were, of course, growing up too, and staying loyal to their favourite group. Fans who were just 13 when Take That started were now almost 20. And the difference was obvious.

'Things have changed for us but they have also changed for our audience,' said Howard. 'I know our fans have grown up because the bras they are hurling on stage these days are much bigger than they once were!'

And while the boys were growing up, their

earnings were growing too. Manager Nigel Martin-Smith revealed to me that Take That were earning an astounding £1 million a month. In fact he admitted that he was constantly turning down all kinds of money-making offers including lucrative film and TV work because it couldn't pay as much as the band were making. Said Martin-Smith, 'We are offered all kinds of projects all the time, including film and TV work, but we have to turn them down because frankly they are not worth it. In the amount of time we would have to take off to do that kind of work, say three months, the band could have made £3 million.'

One such offer, however, caught Take That's imagination. The band were offered the chance to frolic in the Californian sun with curvy Pamela Anderson on the hit US show Baywatch. Nigel Martin-Smith explained, 'The idea is that the boys will be making a video on the beach.'

It seemed an appealing prospect at first. The band and management thought that an appearance on Baywatch would give a boost to their profile in the States, something that was very much on their minds. 'We realise how hard America will be to crack,' said Howard, 'but we're going to give it everything.'

The thought of appearing in their swimwear on

the sun n' sand show had made the guys work out vigorously – especially Gary. He admitted, 'One of the things that made me go on a diet was when I saw that chubby, horrible Spitting Image puppet of me on TV. I know that if I have to appear on the show in my swimwear I've got to look fit. Now I am on a very strict diet which includes cutting out anything with sugar and all dairy food. Jason, who is the health nut in the band, has been making sure that I stick to my diet. It is very hard because I am a real glutton for food. I just love it. I eat everything that's bad for me – chocolate, the lot. In the past I have really mistreated my body.'

But by the time the band were on their European tour they had begun to take the mickey out of Pamela Anderson. Gary said, 'She's plastic. I haven't seen an episode of the show yet.' While Jason agreed, 'I'm not really into Pam. I'm not into plastic.' In the end, Take That's Baywatch frolic bit the dust. The band decided to scrap their appearance on the show because they had to add other dates on their Australian and Far East tours.

'Back For Good' came from the band's new album 'Nobody Else'. To finish the album on time, the band had worked long hours in Gary's home studio in Manchester, relaxing in between singing and playing by sitting out in Gary's garden. 'It was great fun doing the album and it was done very quickly actually - it just took two months,' said Gary. 'This is the most I've ever been involved in an album because I co-produced everything on it.'

On 31 March the band premiered the album to a select group of media folk, including myself. It proved to be very different from the bands earlier albums, showing a new sophistication in song-writing and production. 'Nobody Else' is a fantastic mix of styles, from big ballads such as 'Holding Back The Years' to up-tempo swingbeat songs such as 'Sunday to Saturday' and hip hop numbers such as 'Lady Tonight'. For me the highlights are 'Back For Good', 'Never Forget', 'The Day After Tomorrow', 'Hate It' and 'Every Guy'. Like the single 'Back For Good' this album embraced a wider audience for Take That and was critically acclaimed. *The Times* described Gary as 'a new George Michael in the making'.

The album's title track, 'Nobody Else', was inspired by Gary's parents, who steered his career in the early days. 'I decided to write a song for them one day when they were looking through old photographs of themselves,' he explained. 'I was very touched and wanted to write a song about undying love and devotion.'

When 'Nobody Else' was released on 1 May, it sold an astounding 250,000 copies in Britain alone in just one week, going straight to number one in the album charts. David Joseph, a spokesman for the band, said, 'The album has been selling like crazy. In the first three days we notched up sales of 180,000. Take That are gathering new fans by the day. the band's previous album 'Everything Changes', has gone rocketing back in the chart, too and that's because older buyers have been snapping that up after getting turned on to the band by their latest songs.'

Everything seemed to be going right for Take That, but during the band's European tour in March to April there had been a couple of nasty mishaps. The first came when one of the group's acrobatic dance routines went wrong during a show in Berlin. Howard was left writhing in agony, his finger broken, after falling during a back flip. He was rushed backstage were he was given painkillers and oxygen and had his finger put in a splint. But after missing several numbers Howard came back on stage, to the delight of the fans, after telling the First Aid workers, 'I want to go back on'.

The brave star managed to finish the show, but

immediately it was over he was rushed to the nearest hospital amid fears that the band might have to cancel the tour. A group source told me, 'Howard was in real agony. It was horrible. Everyone was really worried. His finger looked as if it was hanging off. It was bent right back.'

Fortunately doctors managed to put Howard back together again almost immediately and the tour carried on without even one show having to be postponed. Added the source, 'Luckily the band had a number of days off after Berlin and Howard was back on stage for the next date in Kiel. But he won't be able to do back flips or anything like that. We have had to change the routines around.'

After the dramatic accident Howard said, 'I have never known pain like it. I was in absolute agony. But I wanted to get back on stage. I don't like to let the other guys or our fans down.'

Next a gun scare during a concert in Frankfurt led to the band cutting short their show. The drama happened after security men were confronted by a man wielding a gun outside the city's Festival Hall as the concert took place. Take That were immediately alerted to the drama and told not to do an encore. While thousands of fans waited for them to come back on stage they were given an armed guard for protection and bundled

into a waiting ambulance with blackened windows which sped them off to the police headquarters.

After being turned away twice by concert doormen because he did not have a ticket, the gunman had brandished his weapon at two security guards, muttering that he was still going to see the concert. He managed to give both guards and the police the slip, causing panic and setting off a full security alert. The next day security was stepped up at the hall, where the band were playing a second sell-out show, in case the gunman reappeared.

A spokesman for the Frankfurt police said, 'We are still actively looking for the man. We know that he did not have a ticket for the show.' Police spokesman Karl-Heinz Wagner added, 'We feared the worst when we heard this armed man was probably running around outside.'

Take That were badly disturbed by the incident. A representative of the band said, 'Apparently the man was an escaped prisoner and had what appeared to be a machine gun. As a precaution the band have employed armed guards to protect them, with the full co-operation of the police. We do not believe this man was after the band, but the management wanted to make sure that this did not spoil the pleasure of the fans, or the band.' 'We want to tell fans that the band are perfectly safe and enjoying their tour,' said Nigel Martin-Smith. 'We have taken all the necessary steps to ensure the band are safe.'

Europe was going Take That crazy. Every day the tour buses which the group travelled in were completely covered by raunchy and romantic messages from the fans – about 500 messages in all – which were cleaned off every couple of days. The messages said all kinds of things, from 'Mark: Take Me I'm Yours' to 'Jason, let me thrill you till we're both satisfied'. But mostly the messages, which came complete with the girls' home phone numbers, pledged their undying love and devotion. A band source told me, 'The European fans are as wild as the British ones. They will do anything to get to the band.'

Despite a few brief flings and all the offers of love, however, not one of the boys had had a steady girlfriend during the whole time the band have been going. 'We just haven't got the time,' explained Mark Owen. 'We all miss having steady relationships. But I believe that we will all one day have them. I still want to be married by the time I'm 25, though I realise that's not that far off now.'

It was a situation that was soon to change. Take That's new mature music and image had also led to a more mature feelings and a franker approach

to romance. In April 1994 they admitted that in the past they had been worried about having girlfriends and being linked with anyone steady. Now they said they no longer worried about that. Jason and Howard Donald both admitted that they were in relationships with girls back home – though these were open 'arrangements' which meant they were free to see other girls. Jason admitted he had been seeing a lot of sexy telly presenter Jenny Powell, while Howard said he was very fond of a fitness instructor back in Manchester called Vicki.

Mark confessed that he once considered leaving the band for six months because he wanted to fall in love and knew that real love and a proper relationship could only come if you had time to nurture it. He said that he still thought a lot about getting married and was worried that he might have already met the right girl but might not know it because he never had enough time to work a proper relationship out.

The boys were also much more honest about sex. Mark admitted that every girl the band romance knows the score and that they never fool anyone they fancy having a fling with that they are after a proper relationship. Mark added, 'Another strict rule that we have is that every girl we ever go out with has to be over the age of consent. A lot of girls look much older than they really are but we always make a point of knowing exactly how old they are.'

Earlier in the year I had revealed that Robbie had a crush on pretty actress Lisa Walker. In line with the band's wholesome and clean-cut image, however, the cheeky singer had claimed that his love life had been wrecked because he was in Take That. Now he changed his tune. 'I'm a young bloke who has thousands of girls screaming at him,' he confessed. 'I'd be a complete berk if I'd didn't try to make the most of it.'

As Gary Barlow explained, the band were once worried that any smear on their wholesome image - even a minor 'indiscretion' like Robbie being spotted in a nightclub – might wreck their career. Now those worries were now a thing of the past. These days things were much more relaxed and honest when it came to love. He revealed that he would love to romance a girl in every country that the band visited. Considering Take That's soaring world-wide success that would be a lot of young women!

Like Mark, Gary dreamed of settling down and getting married, but he had his own reasons for caution. As writer and co-producer of all the band's songs Gary is the richest member of Take

That. But despite being worth an estimated £5 million – the rest of the band are said to be worth about £1.5 million each – he has a reputation for being tight with money. 'The one thing that has always preyed on my mind is that some girl would make me fall in love with her, marry me and then take me for half my money,' he admitted. 'I am very wary of that and I'm determined it won't happen.'

While Take That were enjoying their sixth number one with 'Back For Good' in April, the band had hammered out a new contract with their record label RCA, said to be worth £20 million. The contract which was for a four album deal meant that the group would get £1 for every CD or tape sold. 'Not that long ago lots of people were saying that we would be splitting up,' said Gary. 'This shows how far from the truth that was.'

In May 1995 'Nobody Else' was released and shot straight to number one in the album charts. It was the crowning glory of a six-year career that read like a fairy story. Take That's three albums 'Take That and Party', 'Everything Changes' and 'Nobody Else' had sold an amazing 7 million records between them around the world. By the end of May those albums had also generated six number one singles and the hopes were that

'Nobody Else' would yield even more and end up selling 5 million copies. The band also had mantelpieces full of awards including three BRIT, two Ivor Novello awards and 23 *Smash Hit* ones.

Gary, Mark, Jason, Robbie and Howard seemed to have everything going for them. To the fans they appeared happier than ever during the balmy summer of 1995. Little did they realise the tragedy that was about to unfold.

BYE BYE BABY

Robbie leaves Take That

The melon he had been carrying fell to the floor with a splat as Robbie flung himself into his mum's open arms and hugged her tight. His grey-green eyes were red from crying and his chirpy voice was flat and sad. 'I'm out of the band, Mum,' the heart-throb singer sobbed. 'I'm not part of Take That anymore.'

July 13 had been the worst day of Robbie's life; a life packed with the kind of fame and fortune other people can only dream about. Now it had all come crashing down around his head. Only a few hours earlier, Robbie had returned from a quick McDonalds lunch to the Cheshire Territorial Army barracks where Take That were rehearsing. He was told that the rest of the band – Gary, Jason, Howard and Mark – wanted to see him. An ominous silence hung in the air as he stood before the four guys with whom he'd spent almost every single day of the last six years. It was broken by words that cut him to the quick. 'We don't want you in the band anymore,' they told him. 'We want you to leave today.' A punch from the world heavyweight champion Mike Tyson couldn't have matched the knockout blow Robbie's pals had just given him.

Robbie was crushed, but he didn't want to show it. Instead he adopted the mask of cockiness that he had worn so often in his role of the group clown. Grabbing a melon that was lying on the fruit tray beside the band, he looked at them coolly and said, 'Is it OK to take this with me when I go?' With that he sauntered away, walking out on the band that had made him one of the biggest pop idols Britain has ever seen.

He was still smiling when he got into the luxury car that waited to take him home at the end of each day. But the smile on his face concealed the anguish and pain that he felt in his heart. Puzzled at his early departure, his driver, Chris, and security man, Paul, asked what time they should pick him up the next day. Robbie put his arms round the melon and pressed it towards him unconsciously. You won't need to pick me up tomorrow,' he told them. 'In fact, you won't need to pick me up ever again. I'm not in the band anymore. I won't be coming back.'

*

On 17 July the world heard that Robbie had left Take That. It seemed impossible to believe. Robbie was an integral part of the band, with a great singing voice to match his good looks. He had sung lead vocals on two of the band's biggest hits 'Could It Be Magic' and 'Everything Changes' and was an accomplished dancer whose acrobatic skills made Take That's performances come to life.

Robbie was the band's biggest personality, the clown of the combo, guaranteed to make any Take That appearance unforgettable, whether it was a TV interview or a stage show. His lightning-fast quips and jokes made the fans fall instantly and madly in love with him – in polls he and the band's cutest member, Mark Owen, regularly emerged as the group's most popular members. The news was totally baffling. Why would he leave the band that had made him a millionaire at only 21 and was set to rake in millions more for him? He was famous, he was adored by girls everywhere, he seemed to be deliciously happy and to have everything he wanted. What's more, Robbie had walked out just two weeks before the most lavishly organised tour of the band's six-year career was about to begin.

For the millions of fans trying come to terms with the fact that Take That were no longer the Fab Five, there were worries, heartaches and fears.

Did Robbie's departure from Take That mean the end of the group? Would the band replace Robbie with a new member? And if so whom? And the fans' anxiety about Robbie were made all the worse because the star had mysteriously disappeared. Many fans were desperate and some even threatened to end their lives over what was the most shocking, depressing and tragic day in Take That's career. Helplines were quickly set up to deal with hysterical girls but some were simply inconsolable. One fan ended up in hospital after taking an overdose of sleeping pills.

When the news broke that the original Take That had died, Robbie took full responsibility for his departure but said little to explain it. He stated that, 'It was an incredibly hard decision to make and I hope the fans understand. I owe everything to them. I have decided to call it a day but I have very positive memories of Take That.' Touching on his relationship with the rest of the band, he added, 'Everything is entirely amicable. I just feel the time is right to go solo.'

Little more could be gleaned from the short statement of Take That's manager, Nigel Martin-Smith, who had steered the boys into becoming the most popular group in Britain. It said only that Robbie was leaving the band immediately and

would not be performing with the rest of the band when they launched into their upcoming tour.

A few days later, Gary Barlow and Mark Owen came forward to put at least some of the fans' fears to rest. In a revealing interview on Radio 1, Gary and Mark told their version of Robbie's heart-breaking departure and how it affected the band. Mark described how Robbie had broken the news that he wished to leave the band to them several weeks earlier. 'Since then we've been talking every day deciding what we should do and which road we should take. But at the end of the day we're all very happy about what's going on and we still believe there's a lot of life left in Take That,' he concluded.

Mark admitted that their immediate decision was to split, but Gary quickly jumped in to explain what made them change their minds. 'What hit us soon after that was that we all still love the business we're in. You're in it for such a short time and we're not ready to go yet. Robbie's chosen to go it alone, but we want to go on as Take That.'

During the Radio 1 interview it emerged that Robbie had a six-month notice period in his contract which meant he could have been made to stay with the group for six months after he first informed them of his decision to leave, to ensure that the band would not be severely and immediately disrupted by his departure. Yet Robbie did not stay for his six-month notice period, which would have meant him taking part in Take That's imminent British tour, as well as important trips to Australia and America. Instead he was out of the band only weeks after he first talked to them about a split. Mark Owen agreed that the timing of Robbie's departure couldn't have been worse, saying, 'The tour is a big pressure point for us as a band, and with a new single, there's a lot going through.'

At first Robbie was to honour the six-month notice period and the fivesome rehearsed for several weeks for the new tour before the dramatic decision was taken for him to go immediately. 'It was obvious that Robbie wasn't very happy,' explained Mark, 'so we got together and decided that as mates we didn't want to put him through the pain for six months and that maybe he should go now.'

Gary made it clear that there was going to be no new member of Take That. 'We're not even thinking of getting someone to take Robbie's place. That would be impossible.' He also added that if Robbie ever changed his mind about leaving the band, the door would always be open for him to come back.

It seemed from what Robbie and the band were saying that the split was an amicable one. But as the weeks unfolded it became clear that this was a long way from the truth. The first obvious hints that the break-up was more troubled came a few days later in a letter that Robbie wrote to the *Sun* newspaper, in which he claimed that he had wanted to carry on in the band till the end of the year but the rest of the group had decided he should leave immediately.

Revealing for the first time some of the reasons for his decision to leave, he wrote, 'Some weeks ago I reached the stage where I had to make a decision to see an end to the pressure I was under from the constant touring and the strict regime of the group. I told them that I would be leaving the band in October when my contract ended but would love to honour my commitment to the band and the fans by completing our forthcoming tour of Britain, Australia and the Far East. Unfortunately the other members of the band felt that I was no longer able to give Take That the long-term commitment they needed and that it would be best if I left the band immediately. The last thing I want to do is to destroy a relationship with friends (i.e. the fans who have offered me love and support for a long time). At the moment I am very scared and confused. I feel that it is of very great importance that I must apologise to everybody who feels let down by the decision for me to leave the band.'

In the letter, Robbie put on a brave face in what was obviously a devastating and unhappy situation. He even managed, in his usual way, to crack a few jokes. The letter, he said, had been the hardest thing he had had to write since his GCSE English Exam. He signed off, 'I'll be back soon, everlasting love'.

It was Robbie's first – brief and constrained – attempt to tell his side of the story and to show that everything in Britain's top band was far from hunk dory. To people who knew the band well, however, it had been apparent for some time that all was not well between Robbie, the rest of the band and their management. What had once been such an incredibly tight-knit circle of friends was slowly dissolving as Robbie began to spend more and more time away from them, taking on a new collection of friends better suited, he believed, to the partying, rebellion and wild nights that he craved and loved. It was as if he felt stifled by the wholesomeness and the discipline of the band and yearned for something outside the group that he could put his considerable talents to.

Over a year earlier, in the June of 1994, he

stunned the pop world by turning up at the Glastonbury Festival – the three-day musical event, with its roots in the hippie beliefs of love and peace, that attracted the wildest audience in Britain, who loved getting rocked and wrecked. In the middle of the fields where fans pitched their tents to enjoy music that was a million notes away from Take That's, was Robbie, having the time off his life. A few weeks later Robbie kicked Take That's clean-cut image into touch by getting his black hair butchered and shaved completely to the skull, making him look, to some minds, like a demented skinhead. Robbie had started going out more and more to clubs with a new set of friends and the rumours began circulating in the pop world that he was partying heavily.

Certainly, in the spring of 1995, when I was one of a few British writers invited to Munich to talk to the band and celebrate their successful European tour, the signs of strain between Robbie and the rest of the band were obvious. At the unveiling of the band's new album, 'Nobody Else', it was revealed that Robbie had not sung any lead vocals at all on the record. When asked why, Robbie joked ironically, 'I haven't done any singing because I'm not any good. My voice broke and I'm out of the band. I've now got a job at a supermarket stacking shelves.' The more serious Gary brushed aside the jokes and gave more of an insight to what was happening behind the scenes. 'We gave Robbie twelve songs to learn and he didn't do any of them,' he stated openly. Trying to be a little more honest, Robbie admitted, 'It's the truth. I just wasn't that good. My lead vocals weren't that great during the time we were making the album. But that has given me a good kick up the backside to make sure I get it together for the next album.'

I chatted to Robbie a number of times during the trip to Munich – in the bar of the luxury hotel where we were both staying and at the swanky party after one of their Munich shows. Though in good spirits he seemed at times rather withdrawn, as if pondering his future. He told me that he wanted to do a number of things outside of the band, though quickly added this would be at a later stage, and it was crystal clear that he felt his talents lay not just in singing and dancing but in a wide variety of fields, such as acting, TV presenting and comedy. As I revealed shortly after that Munich trip, Robbie had been offered the part of boy wonder Robin in the new Batman film, 'Batman Forever', but Nigel Martin-Smith had turned it down because he felt it would get in the

way of what the band were first and foremost about – pop music.

One of the first things that Robbie told me when we met in Munich was that he had heard I was leaving the *Daily Mirror*. None of the other band members brought it up at all as we chatted late into the night and it did not take an amateur psychologist to realise that the thought of quitting was preying on his mind.

As if to underline this, at an after-show party during the tour, Robbie insisted on playing his favourite record – the Sid Vicious version of Frank Sinatra's 'My Way'. When Robbie sang along to the lines 'And now, the end is near, and so I face the final curtain' the message he was giving seemed clear.

Robbie was later to admit that during that European tour he had begun to feel dreadfully unhappy, despite the magic of the stage performances and the adulation of the fans. There were many times when Robbie did not hang out with the rest of the band but was away with his own crowd doing his own thing.

During our chats, Robbie was beginning to question his life in the band and admitted he was desperate to seek new opportunities. 'Once you've had a number one and then another number one and even a massive number one you start thinking, what next? Where's the challenges, what's the point of it all?' he admitted. 'We are all looking for new challenges. We have to keep moving on. I would love to do some acting and I am sure that will come. I can see us taking a break from each other to do various projects for a year. There's always been more to me than just Take That. I want to do so many other things.'

Robbie talked of the restrictions and difficulties of life in Take That, revealing the enormous pressures they were all under. 'There can be times in this band where I just feel I am back at school,' he said. 'After all, I joined Take That when I was 16 and so I really haven't had a chance to do lots of the normal things other teenagers do. Yes, it is great fun, don't get me wrong, but you don't have a lot of time for yourself. Being in a band like this must be a lot like being in the army. You have to get up at a certain time, eat certain things, go out when you're told. Everything is planned. Every second is accounted for. During this tour we even had to phone each other up the night before to make sure we didn't wear the same things during the day when we were doing interviews or meeting record company people.'

'One of the frustrations is that you do get offered

lots of different things because you are in the band but you can't do them because you have your commitment to the band. But I definitely want to have a go at acting – everyone tells me I'd be good.' Then, realising he could be making waves by not toeing the strict party line, he quickly added, 'But that break is way down the line. Take That is the main thing and Take That will be around as long as the fans want us.'

In an open confession of the divide that was growing between him and the others, which hinted of rebellion around the corner, he added, 'I'm not like the rest of the band and at times I really get bored out of my brains. I don't like being told what to do or what to wear. It's like being at school.'

This rebellion was soon to manifest itself extremely publicly, during Take That's appearance on MTV's Most Wanted programme. Fans were able to see for themselves just how wild Robbie's behaviour was getting and how the rest of the band and their manager were becoming concerned by it when the cheeky star dropped his trousers and proceeded to moon for the cameras.

Robbie's strip happened when presenter Ray Cokes asked each member of the band if they would ever pose naked. Bleached blond Robbie stunned everyone by saying he would do it and what was more, he would do it for a 'tenner'. Immediately a member of the audience dared Robbie to carry out his boast by saying she had ten pounds. Mark Owen tried to stop Robbie from baring his buttocks by saying that Williams would only do it if the ten pounds were in old one pound notes, but Robbie cut him short saying, 'No, I'd do it for a new ten pound note. As long as it's ten pounds I don't care.' Then he amazed the audience on the show and its millions of viewers by snatching the money, dropping his trousers and undies to his ankles and showing his backside.

Even anarchic presenter Ray Cokes couldn't believe Robbie's antics and fell to the floor in a mock faint. While Mark, Robbie's best friend in the band, was left speechless, only managing to say, 'Robbie's been a very naughty boy tonight.' As if the strip wasn't bad enough, later on the show, Robbie made veiled references to a famous pornographic film while talking to a young fan.

Robbie's deliberately provocative behaviour was an indication of how tired he was getting of the rigid discipline in the band. It seemed clear that he was becoming embarrassed by his group's way of life because he felt it was too childish and he had outgrown it. Afterwards he seemed hardly

penitent, saying, 'I just got carried away. It was a bit of fun. I like having a laugh.' A friend added more diplomatically, 'Robbie is a great show-off. he hopes he hasn't offended anybody, but he is completely unpredictable. No one ever knows what he is going to do next.'

But Robbie's behaviour was not just something that could be brushed aside as showing-off. It was causing problems for the band, tarnishing their perfect image. One source told me, 'One of the reasons that the band have got where they are is because they have always done what was required and expected of them. They have always obeyed orders and toed the line. But Robbie's unpredictability and rebelliousness is getting out of control and that could damage the band. Not just because it affects their wholesome image but because a band who want to stay at the top have to be extremely disciplined and work hard.'

In the next few weeks Robbie began appearing everywhere, frequently looking rather the worse for wear. It was at this time that drug rumours started surfacing; rumours that he always actively denied. Later, when the news of the split broke, the *Daily Star* claimed that the singer had been sacked because his drug taking was affecting their stage performance. It alleged that Robbie had been taking cocaine and ecstasy and record bosses had tried to persuade him to get help for his problem. The *Star* also claimed that Robbie had been spotted taking cocaine at the Glastonbury Festival and that the singer had confessed to enjoying drugs, allegedly telling them, 'I do loads, you know. I get up to lots. Nobody knows about it.' Robbie hit the roof over the allegations, which he vehemently denies, fuming, 'That one is in the hands of my lawyers. The only plus is that it was in the *Daily Star* and you can't believe everything they write.'

One thing was certain, in the weeks before he and Take That parted company, Robbie was partying like there was no tomorrow. During the weekend of the VE celebrations, he was photographed coming out of one of London's trendiest clubs, The Emporium, with Liverpool goal keeper David James, who like Robbie had his hair bleached and cropped close to the skull. Robbie had been partying so hard that the photographer said he had to be helped into the car by the gangling goalie. A source added, 'Robbie looked rather the worse for wear. He looked as if he had really got into the VE-day spirit. He even made a victory sign.'

Robbie was also seen out with a number of women – something that was against the strict rules imposed by the Take That camp. He was

spotted in a bar passionately kissing a woman who was over ten years older than him. Said one of the guests at the bar, 'They were kissing and cuddling in front of everyone who was there. She was sitting on his lap and they were all over each other. I don't blame him for being so passionate with her. She is stunning looking. She looks like a top model.' Robbie tried to play down his alleged romance with the mum of two saying, 'I do know her but there is no romance between us. She is just part of a large gang I have been hanging out with over the last few months.'

Around this time, it was also revealed that Robbie had a wild night of passion with a pretty 24-year-old German hotel receptionist during the group's European tour. The girl said she and Robbie met up in the hotel bar and she was later brought up to his hotel room by the group's bodyguards. She claimed that Robbie was a great lover and that after their night of romance, she had come to Britain to see him again.

In June, Robbie was back at the Glastonbury Festival where he blackened his tooth to make himself look more gruesome, partied with the rock bands he idolised and got into scrapes with other festival-goers. The clean-cut image that had been so carefully nurtured around Take That just didn't fit in here. The reaction of his peers was crucial to someone as young as Robbie and he found it hard when his new friends teased him about being in the teen idol group.

'At Glastonbury people looked at me as if I was a big pimple on the end of their nose because I'm a member of Take That,' he admitted, obviously stung. 'They think I'm a total prat.' One close source said, 'I think Robbie felt embarrassed about being in Take That, especially because of the strictness around the band and the fact that you couldn't party late and have girlfriends. Robbie often wished he was in more credible bands like Oasis whose music he really liked. I think that was a lot to do with the fact that he was the youngest member of the band and so was more vulnerable to peer pressure.'

Gary had previously hinted at the pitfalls of being the youngest member of such a famous band when he said, 'I do worry about Robbie sometimes. He's the youngest and more so than any of us he has had to do his growing up in the public eye and that can be so hard. The rest of us had time to sow our wild oats before we joined the group so we were able to get that out of our system.'

That second visit to Glastonbury, in June 1995, proved the turning point with the band. From then on the group felt that Robbie's face didn't fit

anymore. He was given a telling-off by manager Nigel Martin-Smith for attending the festival and being pictured with brothers Noel and Liam Gallagher of top Manchester band Oasis. The pair had become good friends with Robbie, who loved the music they made and adored their rebellious, devil-may-care attitude. There had even been talk that he and Oasis would make a record together. But being seen with Oasis, who hit the headlines with their wild behaviour, hotel wrecking, drug-taking and swearing, was considered the wrong image for a Take That star.

Robbie was livid about the scolding. 'I refused to accept a telling-off,' he said later. 'I didn't see that I had done anything wrong. But they were furious because they didn't reckon it was right for the image of the band and about a week or so later they decided to get rid of me.'

It all seemed a million miles away from the time when Robbie had enthusiastically confessed, 'The lads are like my family – they are the people I want to love and who give me love. I don't know what I would do if one of them died. We're that close I might think about ending it myself, too.'

Robbie's letter to the *Sun* on had uncovered flaws in the official story of an amicable split. While Gary

Barlow claimed the group would welcome Robbie back with open arms, Robbie was now saying that he had been pushed out before the tour. Something, somewhere was badly wrong.

Things deteriorated further when, on 9 August, Robbie launched a legal battle to get compensation for missing out on the band's lucrative tour and the merchandising associated with it. Take That tours are a real money-spinning venture. The band makes a fortune from sales of merchandise such as T-shirts and programmes. Music industry sources say that Robbie could have made around £1 million from the tour.

Robbie released a hard-hitting statement through his solicitor, condemning the management of Take That for their handling of the split. 'For some time Robbie Williams has become concerned with the way the band has been developing and the way the management was allowing the band, and in particular Robbie Williams, to grow,' it read. 'He had discussed his concerns with other members of the band and the management. However he has received no positive feedback from either the management or most of the band members. Despite this, Robbie Williams said he would be prepared to fulfil his commitment to the band and the fans throughout 1995, which meant

he would have participated fully in the UK tour and other tours planned for later this year. All the band and management agreed to this proposal. Much to his surprise, half-way through rehearsals for the UK tour he was asked by the band and management not to participate further in the tour at all, which was a decision taken without consultation or discussion with him. Robbie Williams felt he had no alternative, however disappointing it would be to the fans, but to accept his exclusion from participation in the tour . . . It is regretted that the management's involvement in the band's decisions with reference to Robbie Williams has not been even-handed.' In the statement, Robbie made a point of apologising to his fans and thanking them for standing by him since that 'traumatic' July day. The statement continued, 'He will not let his fans down and has been overwhelmed by their support. He hopes shortly to provide positive news of what he will be doing in the future which will fully satisfy the hopes and expectations of his fans.'

A friend of Robbie's made his new position quite clear. 'Robbie was sacked. There was no friendly discussions between him and the rest of the group as they claim.'

Take That hit back immediately, saying, 'When

we saw the statement we were extremely upset. Over the past few months, and most noticeably in rehearsals, Robbie was unable to give us and the fans the long-term commitment we deserve. It was agreed by all five of us that the best thing to do was for him to leave the band to pursue a solo career. It is a great shame that after all the love and the good times we have shared together, this has now become a media issue. We are being asked to say negative things about him, but that will never happen. We will always love him as a friend and whatever he says and does he will always have our complete support.'

But while the band was expressing love for Robbie, behind the scenes the ex-Take Thater was becoming a non-person. Almost every single mention and picture of him had been obliterated from the band's forthcoming official annual. The history of Britain's most successful teen band was being hastily rewritten as Robbie was unceremoniously scrapped from the book. A source revealed, 'The new annual, one of the most important items in the group's merchandising, had been virtually finished when it was suddenly declared that Robbie wasn't to be in it anymore. All the fans who love Robbie will be devastated.'

At the same time organisers preparing the

merchandising for the band's upcoming August tour were busy manufacturing new items containing only the four remaining members of the band. And when the band's new album, 'Nobody Else', was released in America, it was as if Robbie had never existed; all traces of him were removed from the CD cover and booklet, though two credits remain, the first as a vocalist and the second as co-writer on 'Sure'.

The first test for the new four-piece Take That came two weeks after the announcement of Robbie's departure, with the release of their new single, 'Never Forget'. It was, perhaps, one of the most important records of their career; its success or failure would tell them how the fans had reacted to Robbie's departure. Any worries the boys might have had about the fans' loyalties were dispelled when the single shot straight to number one – the seventh time one of their singles had gone straight to the top spot. The band were ecstatic and Gary Barlow immediately thanked the fans for standing by them. 'This has been a hard two weeks for us but once again the fans have been wonderful and have really pulled us through. We'd like to thank you all.'

The next test for the new Take That was the UK

tour. They had generously offered a refund to any fans who were disappointed that Robbie was no longer in the band, if they wanted to return their tickets. Few did so and the series of dates was a resounding success, proving to everyone that the band could survive without the joker in their pack.

The tour was different to anything the band had done in the past. This time the fans came to the band and not the band to the fans. The spectacular stage show was so enormous that it would have been impossible to move around the country, and the band were simply too busy to take part in a long gruelling tour. Instead of trekking all over the country, as they had done in the past, the band only played two venues – one in Manchester, where they kicked off the tour and the other in London's vast Earl's Court Stadium. Around 1,500 special coaches were hired to bring in fans from all over the country – equal to a convoy twelve miles long, covering a distance of over five million miles. A spokesman for the band claimed that the exercise was the greatest single movement of people in the UK since World War II.

The show lived up to all expectations, even without Robbie, their number one clown. Despite all the stress, strain and pressure that the band had been under, the group put on a spectacular show

– a mixture of their classic old hits and the new songs of their much acclaimed new album. Their performances at the 20 sold-out dates, which saw them play to 300,000 people, were all the more impressive because everything – from the complicated dance routines to the lead vocals – had to be changed in just a few days because of Robbie's departure.

The concerts showed a new maturity in Take That. Two of the most talked about items were the band's cover versions of Nirvana's grunge anthem 'Smells Like Teen Spirit' and Pink Floyd's anti-school classic 'Another Brick In The Wall', both songs associated with an older, more sophisticated audience. Ironically this was the kind of material that Robbie Williams loved and when he talked about a change of direction for Take That, this is the kind of music he would have had in mind. Ironically, too, these songs were originally to have been sung by Robbie. It was a sharp change of style for Take That but the foursome performed the two songs well and as with their Beatles medley, it introduced their audience to a different kind of music. The band were showing the critics who dismissed them as just another teen band that there was much more to them than a few soppy songs which made young girls hysterical. Like the

Beatles in the sixties, they were progressing from teen idols to mature pop stars.

The rest of the show contained a lot of familiar old magic as well as some brand new sparkle. The band had reached a new peak. They managed to make the older more familiar songs like 'Could It Be Magic' come out as fresh as the day they were first sung by giving them new treatments, while numbers like 'Pray' and 'Babe' retained their power through sheer emotion. The songs from the new album were received rapturously, especially 'Back for Good' and 'Never Forget', the latter a magnificent spectacle sung on a moving walkway which kept them rooted to the same spot though they walked forward, hundreds of lights flashing around them.

There was still plenty of raunch left in the performance and the rapport with the audience was better than ever. At one point in the show a fan was whisked up from the vast ground to flirt sexily with the band, receive a romantic gift of flowers and chocolates and be serenaded by Gary with 'A Million Love Songs'.

The success of the tour boosted moral in the Take That camp. Gary, who had worked-out tirelessly, losing pounds so he could wear the special devil and angel costumes, said, 'Of course I'm

disappointed about what happened, because to me Take That has always been the five of us. But I am getting used to it now and I think the others are too. Time is a great healer. Besides we have a lot of things that we still haven't done and which we want to succeed in. If you want us we are going to be around for a long time yet. We could be around in five years' time. Of course we had our doubts at first about how life would be as a four-some but the fans as ever have been wonderful and got rid of any doubts and worries we might have had. They really lifted us.' Jason added, 'Robbie's leaving has made us even stronger. We are determined to get better and better. I was very nervous about doing a lot more singing at first but I soon settled into it.'

A few days before the tour finished, Robbie and the new Take That came face to face for the first time since the split. It was an emotional moment. The occasion was the National Television Awards, a prestigious showbiz event. The four members of Take That were there to collect an award on behalf of Top of the Pops which was voted The Best Young Persons' Show, while Robbie was there to present the Most Popular Newcomer award to Coronation Street actress Angela Griffin, who plays Fiona Middleton.

Though the guys saw each other, they communicated only by a perfunctory wave. It was evidence of how deep the rift had become. Trying to shrug it off, Robbie said, 'I didn't speak to them in words, it was just hand signals. But that doesn't bother me. When I was in the band we would often just talk in monosyllables.' But Robbie's old mate Mark was more candid about the feelings it raised. 'It was obviously emotional seeing him,' he said, 'but we're getting on with our lives.'

However much he might try to hide it, it was emotional for Robbie, too, and later he was spotted wandering around backstage in tears. 'It's just hard seeing them,' he finally admitted. 'It feels so weird. But I know I've got to start a new life.' He cheered himself up by flirting with many of the beautiful actresses there and later at London's Browns night club. Among the celebrity women that he flirted with were EastEnders stars Patsy Palmer and Martine McCutcheon, Neighbours beauty Natalie Imbruglia, Claudia Schiffer, Michelle Collins and Dani Behr.

Recovering his sense of humour, Robbie joked, 'I was feeling a bit low so I decided to cheer myself up by kissing as many beautiful women as I could lay my hands on. I'm lucky because I can get away

with it, most fellas would get a slap in the face if they tried what I've just done.'

When the producers of Channel 4's Big Breakfast heard of Robbie's split from Take That, they immediately put in an offer. He had done a stint as a guest presenter on the show before, and proved a natural, would he come back for a week? Four weeks later he appeared on the programme, giving his first interview since the split.

Robbie poked fun at his old mates and their wholesome lifestyle saying that while he enjoyed partying, they had become staid stay-at-homes. The star, who admitted he had been partying ever since he and the band parted company, said, 'It was like I was Lemmy from Motorhead [a fast-living hard rocker] and they were Andy Pandys. No, I'm only joking. They rock and roll; they party. It's just that they drink camomile tea, don't you Mark?' It was a pointed dig at the band's clean-living lifestyle.

Robbie was obviously revelling in his new-found freedom from the hard work and tough rules of Take That. 'Now I can go to the loo without a security guard in attendance,' he joked. 'I'm free. I'll be going out for a few nights now. I've started celebrating and I haven't stopped yet. Make-up had an awful time covering the bags under my eyes this morning.'

The star said hello to Jason, Howard and Mark, but tellingly made no mention of Gary, the brains and driving force behind the group. Gary is the member of the band closest to manager Nigel Martin-Smith and between them they set the pace, the style and the rules of Take That. Robbie would later say that despite being in a band with him for six years, he hardly knew Gary at all.

Hundreds of loyal fans descended on the Big Breakfast's East London studio to mob the singer, proving his popularity had not waned since the split.

In the weeks that followed, Robbie opened up more and more to the media. There was no doubt in his mind that he had been sacked. He described how he was left in floods of tears and felt horribly alone when the band told him they didn't want him to tour with them anymore. Being with Take That had become like serving time in prison and that imprisonment was ruining his mental health. As the years passed he hated all the constraining rules that he was forced to live by, felt there was hardly any bond between him and the other members – except for Mark – and grew to detest the band's music.

In a revealing interview with the *Sun*, Robbie described how he was given his marching orders while he and the rest of the band were rehearsing for the tour at the Cheshire Territorial Army Centre. Robbie felt he was doing his best during those rehearsals, knuckling down after the band told him that he wasn't pulling his weight. But he could not concentrate fully; his mind kept drifting back to the comfort, love and security of his mum's home.

Reliving that fateful day, Robbie recalled, 'That afternoon the other guys said they had been discussing things on their own and decided that I should go. Jason actually said it. He told me, "We want to prove we can do it as a four-piece now and not later." They told me that they weren't happy with the way I was conducting myself. To say that I was stunned is a bit of an understatement but I didn't want to crumble in front of them.'

Instead Robbie 'crumbled' when he got into the car to be driven home. He confessed, 'When I told Paul the driver and Chris the security man that I was never ever coming back, the car went very quiet and I just had to look away. I had tears streaming down my face. It was a horrible, horrible moment. I just felt abandoned and totally alone.'

Robbie confessed that he was so traumatised by

what happened that he had to go into hiding because he felt so scared. 'For four days I was a trembling blubbering mess,' he admitted. 'But now I am determined to succeeded. I am making my own decisions for the first time in my life, living my own life and feel since being away from Take That I have turned from a boy into a man.'

Robbie had grown tired of the control and conditioning that Nigel Martin-Smith forced onto the band and had come to fear and despise the tellings-off he got in what were euphemistically called 'Behaviour Meetings'. Robbie, who said that the Behaviour Meetings happened after three 'mistakes', revealed that he was the only one of the band who ever got told off. Offences included going out without security guards or being photographed coming out of a pub.

The picture that Robbie painted of Take That was far from the tight-knit band of brothers they had always seemed. 'We were together for six years but I never knew what was going on in the other guys' minds. I didn't like that and I didn't understand it. The fans think they know the guys, but they don't. No one does. We used to say that if we weren't in Take That we would still have been mates, but I don't know if that's true. The only one that I knew was Mark. We were close and not being

able to see him is one of the hardest aspects of all this.'

Robbie's revelations gave stunning insights into the behind-the-scenes workings of the Take That camp. The band's management, terrified that any bad publicity might harm the band's wholesome and clean-cut image, laid down strict rules. 'The basic formula for Take That was no girlfriends, no being seen in clubs, not having your picture taken in places you shouldn't be and most important of all – always having to toe the party line,' he explained. Minders shadowed the boys 24 hours a day, even controlling the boys love life, 'I was allowed to have sex,' Robbie said, 'as long as the security guards could bring the girls up to the room.' For the young singer this proved intolerable, he didn't want to look like a Hollywood superstar such as comedian Eddie Murphy whose every step is shadowed by a team of burly bodyguards.

With his new-found freedom, Robbie plans to take back the teenage years he lost as part of Take That and truly be himself. He would like to have a steady girlfriend, something that no member of Take That could have. 'Now if I want sex, I have it. And I'm not bothered if it's in the papers or whatever.'

Certainly Robbie is embarking on a solo career with much panache and style. He seems to be everywhere. He has appeared in an episode of EastEnders, presented Top of the Pops and gone on stage in the West End musical hit 'The Rocky Horror Show'. He is much in demand – he was paid a reputed £100,000 for doing a saucy advert for soft drink 7-Up Light in which he dressed up in drag, donning high-heeled stilettos, a long black wig and bikini bottoms. Tony Mortimer from East 17, who were once Take That's bitterest rivals, told me he would love to write a big smash hit with Robbie, and East 17's manager Tom Watkins agreed he would like Robbie to make some guest appearances with the band. Peter Clark, the MD of Talk Radio UK, told me he would love to have Robbie star in his TV series Bugs.

As I write in late September 1995, Robbie has not yet made his first solo record – though there has been talk of a rap tune and mumblings of a duet with Louise Nurden, who left hit band Eternal at the same time that Robbie bust up with Take That. Certainly he will have plenty of material for solo records – he has notebooks full of poems and lyrics which those in the know say will make great songs. There is no doubt that Robbie will have a string of smash hits because he has not only the

talent but also the determination to succeed. He has tasted success and will be hungry to feast on it again. But I think that music will be just one string to his bow along with acting, TV presenting and comedy, for which he has a natural flair.

And what of Take That? For them it is onward and upward. The world is truly their oyster. The country which they have been determined to conquer, America, has finally succumbed. Their smash hit 'Back For Good' soared up the American charts giving the band their biggest hit ever there. September saw them on another tour of Australia, to be followed by another assault on America which will take them up to the end of 1995. Gary has said that the band has years left in them and Mark, Jason and Howard have all vowed to keep going as long as the fans out there want them to.

Will Robbie and Take That ever perform together again? Who knows. Robbie claims he only got lawyers involved because he wants monetary compensation for not being able to tour with the band this year, and the despite the terrible strain of the situation, there have been no harsh words between him and his former pals. Robbie and the rest of Take That have been keen to point out that there is still a lot of affection between them. You can't just forget six years of your life, especially such formative ones. It would be magic if they did get back together one day, if only for a one-off concert. But if they don't, all those fans who cried their eyes out when they heard about Robbie's split from the world's number one pop band should look on the bright side. After all, now they have TWO fab acts to adore, not just one.

WHAT HAPPENED WHEN

1984 – Jason Orange is in a break-dance crew, Street Machine, while Howard Donald is in a crew called the RDS Royals. Later they join together to form Street Beat.

1987 – Gary Barlow meets Mark Owen at Manchester's Strawberry Studios and they eventually form a group together called The Cutest Rush.

1990 – Both groups meet through Nigel Martin-Smith's Manchester-based entertainment agency. They advertise for a fifth band member and Robbie Williams auditions and gets the job.

September 1990 – Take That formed and sign contract.

March 1991 – The band secures a slot on the BSB show *Cool Cube*.

April 1991 – The band embarks on a regional tour of British clubs.

July 1991 – Take That's debut single, 'Do What U Like', is released on Nigel Martin-Smith's independent label, Dance UK. Single reaches number 82.

Jelly and ice cream video, co-produced by Ro Newton and Angie Smith, is shown on *The Hitman and Her.*

September 1991 – Take That sign a major album deal with RCA after head of A&R Nick Raymond hears about them and sees them perform.

October 1991 – Band undergoes a change of image, dumping the leather look for string vests.

November 1991 – The band's second single, 'Promises', is released and reaches number 38.

Take That appear on *Wogan, Going Live, O-zone, Motormouth* and *Pebble Mill.*

December 1991 to January 1992 – The band complete their LP.

January 1992 – 'Once You've Tasted Love' released. It reaches number 47.

February 1992 – Take That embark on the famous 'Safe Sex' tour, organized in conjunction with the Family

Planning Association. They perform at schools and clubs up to four times a day, along with promo signings.

May 1992 – 'It Only Takes a Minute' is released and reaches number 7. The single marks the first real success for the band.

They appear at the Children's Royal Variety Performance. Princess Margaret says backstage that she loves their saucy dance routines.

June 1992 – The band appear on the Radio 1 Road Show at Alton Towers and receive an incredible reception.

They appear at Crystal Palace for National Music Day.

August 1992 – New single, 'I Found Heaven', is released and reaches number 15.

Debut album *Take That and Party* is released and reaches number 2.

HMV record shop tour begins. Fans besiege the band in London, Glasgow, York and Manchester. HMV cancel the rest of the tour for safety reasons.

October 1992 – 'A Million Love Songs' is released, which rises to number 7.

November 1992 – UK tour begins, taking in major venues throughout Britain.

December 1992 – The band win seven awards in the *Smash Hits* poll: Best Band in the World, Best British Band, Best LP, Best single and Best video. Mark Owen wins awards for Best Haircut and Most fanciable male.

Take That also win eight awards in *TV Hits* magazine readers' poll.

December 1992 – Take That release the video of *Take That and Party*, which rockets to the number 1 spot.

'Could It Be Magic' released, which reaches number 3 in the chart.

January 1993 – Take That nominated for two BRITS awards.

February 1993 – Take That release a new single, 'Why Can't I Wake Up With You'. It storms straight into the charts at number 2. They win Best Single category at the BRIT awards for 'Could It Be Magic'.

April 1993 – Take That make their second assault on America, releasing their British hit single 'It Only Takes A Minute' and their album, 'Take That and Party'.

June 1993 – Gary Barlow appears in an ad for Stimorol chewing gum.

Take That play at Crystal Palace as part of National

Music Day. Fans collapse in the heat, crush and passion of the band's performance.

July 1993 – Take That kick off a brand new, sell-out tour, playing to their biggest ever audiences. 8,000 flock to see them at Manchester's G-Mex.

Take That get their first number one with 'Pray' which shoots straight to the top.

August 1993 – 30 Fans need hospital treatment and 100 need First Aid after the band appear in concert in Chelmsford, Essex. A tragedy is averted when the band stops the show and pleads with the fans to calm down.

The band perform a saucy striptease for the Childline charity in London, dropping their trousers to reveal huge letters spelling out the word Childline on the backs of their undies.

October 1993 – Take That's two-year ban on having steady girlfriends is over.

'Relight My Fire' hits the top spot in the charts.

Their second album, 'Everything Changes' is released. To date the album has sold 3 million copies.

November 1993 – Take That embark on their second British tour.

Take That go into pop history as the first act ever to have three consecutive records go straight to number one when 'Babe' hits the top spot.

February 1994 – The group perform their Beatles homage to a star-studded audience at the BRITS.

March 1994 – Take That set off on a gruelling European tour which includes, Germany, Holland and Sweden.

The title track of the album 'Everything Changes' is released, it soars straight to number one.

May 1994 – Gary wins two trophies for his songwriting at the prestigious Ivor Novello awards.

Rumours race round the world that Mark has cracked under the pressure and has been rushed to hospital. The rumours prove to be false.

June 1994 – 'Love Ain't Here Anymore' is released. It fails to reach number one, but hits the number three spot.

August 1994 – Take That kick off their new tour in Glasgow. The show causes a furore when Howard Donald performs in leather chaps which display his bare backside.

October 1994 – 'Sure' becomes Take That's fifth record to go into the charts at number one.

'Sure' becomes Take That's fifth record to go into the charts at number one.

November 1994 – The band perform in front of Prince Charles at the Royal Variety Show.

December 1994 – Take That perform in front of the Princess of Wales at the Concert of Hope at London's Wembley Arena.

Take That sweep the board in the *Smash Hits* readers poll.

February 1995 – Take That perform their new single 'Back for Good' at the BRITS.

March 1995 – The band kick off a new European tour.

'Nobody Else' is showcased to selected journalists in Munich.

April 1995 – 'Back for Good' goes straight into the charts at number one.

There is a gun drama outside the Take That concert in Frankfurt.

Take That sign a £20 million deal with their record company RCA for four albums.

May 1995 – The third album, 'Nobody Else' is released and sells an astonishing 250,000 copies in just one week.

June 1995 – The band attends the Nordoff Robbins Silver Cleff awards in London. At the auction, soccer-mad Robbie spends £16,000 on an annual season ticket for Wembley. It is the last time the band are pictured together as a fivesome.

July 1995 – Robbie and the rest of Take That have a showdown and part company on the 13th. Four days later it is announced that Robbie Williams has left Take That.

'Never Forget' is released and goes straight to number one.

August 1995 – Take That start their UK tour, without Robbie. Robbie claims he was sacked from the band and starts legal proceedings.

September 1995 – Robbie earns an estimated £100,000 for appearing in drag for a 7-Up Light advertisement.

Take That set off on a tour of Australia and America, taking them to the end of 1995.

QUIZ

Are you a truly dedicated fan? Test yourself and see.

1 **Which northern city do most of the Take That members come from?**

a) Bradford
b) Liverpool
c) Manchester

2 **He started on his first keyboard at only ten. He now writes Take That's songs. Who is he?**

3 **To concentrate on becoming megastars, the guys gave up romance. But for how long?**

4 **One fan said he should do a spread for a sexy magazine, and now his nickname is 'Centrefold'. Who is he?**

5 **Which ballroom dancing competition did Howard's troupe win?**

6 **Who had the nickname 'Baby'?**

7 **When Robbie first started sucking a dummy, what was he hiding?**

a) A spot
b) A black eye
c) A swollen lip

8 **They're no swots and one of the band has admitted he left school without a single O level. Who is he?**

9 **Football crazy Mark tried out for two local teams as a lad. Which were they?**

10 **Mark's mum told him to give up his struggling pop career to become what?**

a) A deep sea diver
b) A bank clerk
c) A dustman

11 **How many people turned up to see the band's first show in Huddersfield?**

a) 200
b) 20
c) 2,000

12 How does manager Nigel keep the guys from getting big-headed?

a) By making them sing nursery rhymes
b) By taking fans home to dinner
c) By making them do the washing-up

13 Their first single, 'Do What U Like', didn't even reach the Top Eighty. How far did it get?

14 Which pint-sized Aussie pop singer did Jason Orange have a crush on?

15 What was the name of the band Gary and Mark formed before Take That?

16 Which member of the band has a sister called Tracy?

17 Whose father was a Latin American dance teacher?

18 What was Take That's first number one single?

19 How long did 'Sure' stay at the top of the charts?

20 Jason has a twin brother. Who is older and by how much?

21 Which now sadly defunct magazine did the band appear nearly nude in?

22 What is Robbie's middle name?

23 What were the guys smeared with during the video for 'Do What U Like'?

24 Who is keen on rollerblading?

25 The guys were smuggled past thousands of fans out of the HMV store in Manchester. What were they wearing as disguise?

a) Police uniforms
b) Gorilla suits
c) Raincoats

26 Which member of Take That loves girls with long dark hair, 'like Yasmin le Bon'?

27 How many songs are there on *Take That and Party*?

28 Which member of the band has a pet lizard called Nirvana?

29 When did the band first sign their contract with Nigel Martin-Smith?

30 Whose mum suffered so badly after one of Take That's concerts that she had to take pills for inflammation of her eardrums?

31 Take That had only one single in the Top Ten before 'I Found Heaven'. What was it?

32 Which seventies band did the original version of 'It Only Takes a Minute'?

33 Which Take That member claimed he went through girlfriends like hot dinners at school, and has never been in love?

34 Which craze in jeans fashion did Take That bring back into style?

35 Take That turned his classic melody 'Could It Be Magic' into an up-tempo hit. Name the middle-aged singer/song-writer.

36 He is going to return the compliment with his own version of which Take That ballad?

37 Jason and Howard break-danced together in another group before Take That. What was it called?

a) Boneshaker
b) Street Heat
c) Street Beat

38 Two members of the band don't come from Manchester. Who are they and where do they come from?

39 What is Jason's favourite motto?

a) Too many cooks spoil the broth.
b) Variety is the spice of life.
c) Don't kill the goose that laid the golden egg.

40 Which rock legend did Mark impersonate as a youngster?

41 Which Take That song features the lyrics 'I found love with somebody else's girl'?

42 What is Robbie's favourite soap?

a) Coronation Street
b) Emmerdale
c) Eldorado

43 Which member of the band had hypnosis to beat his fear of cars?

44 Which member of the band has a dolphin tattoo?

45 How many other youngsters were competing against Robbie to win a place in Take That?

a) 20
b) 200
c) 2,000

46 What was Take That's first American top 20 hit?

47 Name the dark-haired TV presenter Jason was romantically linked with?

48 Which member of the band said, 'I will never grow up and I will never have a proper job'?

49 When Robbie and the band broke up, where were they rehearsing?

50 Who was Robbie's best friend in Take That?

ANSWERS TO QUIZ

1 c
2 Gary
3 Two years
4 Howard
5 *Come Dancing*
6 Robbie
7 a
8 Howard
9 Manchester United and Rochdale
10 b
11 b
12 c
13 Eighty-two
14 Kylie Minogue
15 The Cutest Rush
16 Mark
17 Howard
18 Pray
19 Two weeks
20 Jason, by twenty minutes
21 *No. 1*
22 Peter
23 Jelly and ice cream
24 Robbie
25 a
26 Jason
27 Thirteen
28 Mark
29 September 1990
30 Howard's mum
31 'It Only Takes a Minute'
32 Tavares
33 Robbie
34 Turn-ups

35 Barry Manilow

36 'A Million Love Songs'

37 c

38 Gary (Frodsham, Cheshire) and Robbie (Stoke-on-Trent)

39 b

40 Elvis Presley

41 'I Found Heaven'

42 a

43 Gary

44 Mark

45 c

46 'Back for Good'

47 Jenny Powell

48 Robbie

49 The Territorial Army barracks in Stockport, Cheshire.

50 Mark

HOW DID YOU SCORE?

40 or more	Consider yourself a true super-fan!
20—39	You're obviously a loyal fan, and well on your way to total dedication.
5—19	Could do better – some extra Take That homework might be in order.
Under 5	Call yourself a fan? Are you sure we're talking about the same band?

ACKNOWLEDGEMENTS

Many people helped in getting this book together. Among those I would particularly like to single out is Louise Johncox, my researcher, who made an intrepid and invaluable contribution to the book. Other thanks go to Don Short, my agent, and Val Hudson, Karen Whitlock and Jenny Oliver at HarperCollins.

Thanks must also go to all the members of Take That, Gary Barlow, Mark Owen, Robbie Williams, Jason Orange and Howard Donald, who gave me such great interviews, as well as their manager Nigel Martin-Smith and PRs, Loretta de Souza, Jane Chapman and David Joseph. Other people who were helpful include Pete Waterman, Ro Newton and Carolyn Norman.

Hundreds of newspaper and magazine articles were used as secondary sources to my own interviews, including the *Daily Mirror*, the *Sun*, *Smash Hits*, *Music Week*, *Just Seventeen*, *Big*, *TV Hits*,

Sunday Magazine, the *Daily Star*, the *Daily Mail* the *Mail on Sunday*, and the *Daily Express*. Other sources included Radio 1, Capital Radió, O-Zone, Talk Radio and Sky TV.